FLOUR COOKING, NATURALLY

JO SMITH

Hutchinson Benham, London

ACKNOWLEDGEMENTS
Drawings by Gill Zeiner
Photography by Michael Lorenzini
Designed by Mike Rose and Bob Lamb
Food prepared by Barbara Cariss,
Sue Hollingsworth and Hilary Lane

Hutchinson Benham Limited

An imprint of the Hutchinson Group
3 Fitzroy Square, London W1P 6JD

Hutchinson Group (Australia) Pty Ltd
30–32 Cremorne Street, Richmond South, Victoria 3121
PO Box 151, Broadway, New South Wales 2007

Hutchinson Group (NZ) Ltd
32–34 View Road, PO Box 40–086, Glenfield, Auckland 10

Hutchinson Group (SA) (Pty) Ltd
PO Box 337, Bergvlei 2012, South Africa

First published 1980

Photographs © Thorn Domestic Appliances (Electrical) Ltd 1980

Illustrations and text ©Hutchinson Benham Ltd 1980

Set in Plantin

Computerset by MFK Graphic Systems (Typesetting) Ltd
Saffron Walden, Essex
Printed by Hazell, Watson & Viney Ltd, Aylesbury

ISBN 0 09 142631 6

CONTENTS

INTRODUCTION

Flour Cooking, Naturally is both a recipe book and a comprehensive guide to the art of successful flour cookery. The recipes take full advantage of the different varieties of flour available today, and also make use of a special gadget which enables you to mill your own flour, introducing new flavours and textures to your cooking. Each different type of flour, from buckwheat to wholemeal flour, is described, and suggestions are given as to which recipes they suit best. The recipes themselves are collected from all over the world, and include national specialities such as American Anadama bread and Russian Blinis.

Both traditional and modern methods of making bread, cakes, pastry, biscuits and pasta are given. Bread dough, for example, can be made either by handkneading or, if you find that too strenuous, by using a dough hook attachment on your electric mixer. Similarly, if you find it difficult to make pastry by rubbing-in, you can use the beaters on your mixer and be sure of light-as-a-feather results.

Ranging from the exotic to the everyday, all the recipes have been tested by both methods. **Flour Cooking, Naturally** bridges that gap between the time-consuming recipes of our grandmothers' time and today's convenience foods, bringing you home-cooking at its best while taking full advantage of modern labour-saving devices.

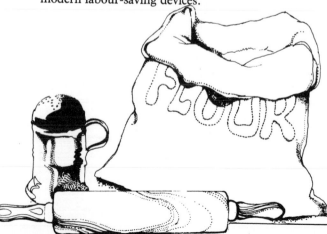

The origins of wheat

Throughout world history, wheat has been used as a form of currency; wheat shortages have led to riots and revolution; control of the wheat supply has been a powerful weapon in the hands of tyrants; failure of harvests has led to famine and disaster.

Wheat was first cultivated more than nine thousand years ago, when men found that wild grains could be collected and stored through winter to ensure a life-saving supply of food. Prehistoric man soon discovered how to cultivate the grain and grind it into a very crude flour by crushing it between stones. By mixing this flour with water and baking the dough in the sun, men produced the first unleavened bread. By the Stone Age, men were flavouring their bread with honey and herbs, and Iron Age men were making a crude form of leavened bread with a mixture of potash liquor and sour milk.

By the time of the Romans, wheat growing and milling methods had improved greatly, and Rome even boasted a college of bakers set up to maintain baking standards. Following the Egyptian custom, the Roman patrician class ate white bread, the ordinary people brown bread, and the unfortunate members of the navy, made up of criminals and renegades, were left with just the bran bread. The Romans introduced large-scale wheat production into Britain and also the circular millstone, which made milling easier. After four hundred years of occupation Britain had become one of the granaries of the Roman empire. The Romans' departure led to the decline of wheat-growing in Britain and it was not until Anglo-Saxon times that wheat was re-established as a major crop.

By the Middle Ages, the water-powered mill had become a central part of the community. Peasants would bring their grain to be milled and the miller would keep back a portion of the grain to pay for his trouble. As most homes lacked ovens, and home-made bread had to be baked in open hearths, bake-houses were set up where the 'huswife' could take her raw bread to be cooked. More often than not the loaves would come back smaller than they should have been, and this led, indirectly, to the setting up of bakery guilds which placed strict controls over unscrupulous bakers. It is no surprise to find that in Tudor times the nobility still ate bread made from the finest flour while the poorer classes ate the bran bread. Elizabeth I had her own special wheat grown to make into 'manchets', a soft white bread made from the finest white flour.

The Georgian Age saw England established as an agricultural nation with a much improved level of wheat production. People still felt that white flour made the most desirable bread. As white flour takes longer to refine, people resorted to adding ground bones and chalk to whiten the flour artificially.

In the nineteenth century the Corn Laws imposed a levy on the wheat which Britain had to import. The result was an insupportable rise in the price of bread, which led eventually to the repeal of the Laws in 1846. As Britain developed into an industrial nation, and its population increased, it became only too clear that domestic wheat harvests would not feed the nation. Extra wheat, therefore, had to be imported, and this situation has continued to the present day.

While bread may support life, people through the ages have used their imagination to vary basic dough recipes. By adding extra flavourings, fats and fruit the first cakes were made. In sixteenth century England, bakers produced spiced breads and buns which were sold for celebrations and special occasions like Christmas and Easter. By the eighteenth century cooks were adding eggs to cakes to make them lighter; one recipe instructs the poor cook to beat the mixture for three hours! Light airy sponge cakes, which are still a treat today, arrived in the nineteenth century with the introduction of chemical baking powders.

With an annual world wheat crop of over 300 million tons obtained from over 30,000 varieties of wheat, we have come a long way from the wild grasses which developed into the primitive wheat of prehistoric times.

Corn

Corn is the collective term for wheat, oats and barley. Corn is described as being either spring corn or winter corn. These terms refer to the time at which the corn is sown or 'drilled'. Corn drilled in the spring grows quickly through the summer and can be harvested later the same year. Winter corn is not, as you might think, drilled in the winter, but in the autumn. It germinates and becomes well established before the cold weather sets in and is harvested at the end of the following summer.

Once you know what to look for, wheat, barley and oats are easy to tell apart. Wheat has hard, compact heads, with the layers of grain tightly packed, giving the appearance of soldiers standing erect. Oats have bell-like ears that hang from slim stems and ruffle with the slightest breeze. Barley has a distinctly whiskered appearance; the heads of the grain hanging down from the necks of the stem.

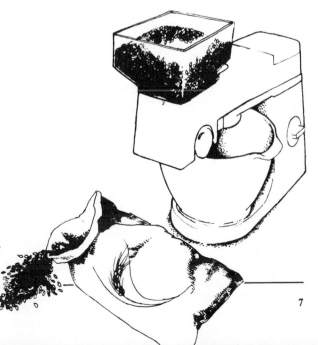

Wheat

A grain of wheat consist of the following:

The germ is the part of the berry which contains the young plant. It contains a high proportion of protein which is important for building and repair of body tissues. It also provides warmth and energy, and vitamins of the B complex which regulate body processes.

The endosperm makes up 85 per cent of the grain and is the main store of carbohydrate, or starch. The carbohydrate also generates warmth and energy.

The aleurone layer is the outer layer of the endosperm, which has a high proportion of protein.

The scutellum is the very thin layer between the germ and the endosperm which contains vitamin B; essential for good health.

The bran is the outer, fibrous covering of the grain. It has a high proportion of cellulose, or 'roughage' as it is often known. This covering is rich in minerals and it fulfils a useful role in aiding digestion and preventing constipation.

In this book, 'flour' generally means flour milled from wheat. It will be clear from the text when the recipe requires other types of flour, such as soya bean flour, lentil flour or buckwheat flour.

Wholemeal, wheatmeal, plain and self-raising flour are milled from wheat. These flours are obtained from two types of wheat known as hard wheats and soft wheats.

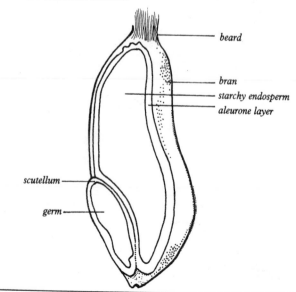

beard

bran
starchy endosperm
aleurone layer

scutellum

germ

Hard wheat is a descriptive term signifying that the grain is physically hard. When milled, these wheats yield 'strong' flours, which have a relatively high protein content. A substance called gluten is formed when water is added to this flour. Gluten is important in bread-making because its elastic qualities allow the gas formed by the yeast to be trapped in the bread, so ensuring a good rise. Hard wheats may be sown in spring or autumn and are grown in the extreme climates of Canada and the USSR, where the grain is sown during the short, hot summer.

Soft wheats are grown in Britain and Northern Europe, where they may be drilled in spring or autumn. Soft wheats produce a flour low in protein which is ideal for cakes and biscuits.

The third category of wheat is known as *durum* or pasta wheat. These grains are even harder than the hard wheats mentioned above. If *durum* wheat was milled to flour fineness, the starch grains would be damaged considerably and so they are usually milled coarsely to produce what we know as semolina.

Modern milling

Traditionally, grain was crushed between stone millstones. Milling methods were changed drastically in the nineteenth century with the coming of the roller mill. This method made it possible to produce a finer flour. Nowadays, after the grain has been cleaned, varying proportions of hard and soft wheat are blended together forming the 'grist'. The resulting flour is never entirely soft or hard, but a mixture of the two. Break rollers open each grain to separate the bran from the endosperm or starchy part. The endosperm is first milled to semolina before being ground into flour and subsequently graded through a series of fine sieves. In the United Kingdom, the resulting flour is chlorine bleached to give the white colour which commercial dough production demands. Bleaching destroys the vitamin E content of the flour. The law stipulates that this, along with vitamins B (thiamine) and B2 (nicotinic acid) must be replaced, and calcium added in the form of chalk.

Most of the bran and wheat germ, or 'offal' as it is known in the trade, is sold as animal feed, although some finds its way into various patent foodstuffs or back into white flour to make certain branded wheatmeal flours.

Extraction rate

When an 'extraction rate' is mentioned on packet flour it means the percentage of the whole grain that remains in the flour after milling. White flour contains usually 70–72 per cent of the wheat grain. 'Patent' flours are produced which have a lower extraction rate, of 40–50 per cent. These are top-grade white flours, and consequently the most expensive. They give the best results in cakes and pastries.

Brown or wheatmeal flour usually contains 80–90 per cent of the wheat grain. Wholemeal flour contains the whole of the wheat grain, from which nothing has been removed and to which nothing has been added. Stoneground flour is wholewheat flour produced by grinding the wheat between millstones rather than through commercial steel rollers.

Storing flour
The best way to store flour is in a cool, dry, airy place. If your kitchen is rather damp and steamy put the flour into a container such as a tin with a lid or a stoppered storage jar. The container should be washed and thoroughly dried before filling with fresh supplies. Do not add new flour to old. Plain flour should keep well for four to six months; self-raising flour for two to three months. Because of the oil content from the wheatgerm, wholemeal flour may go rancid if stored incorrectly, or kept too long. Wholemeal or wheatmeal flours should be stored in a cool dry place away from other flours. They can be kept for up to two months. It is best to buy flour in small quantities or mill your own as and when required.

Milling wheat at home
If you own either a Kenwood Chef or Major mixer you can mill your own wheat at home with the Wheat Mill attachment. It is suitable for both hard and soft wheats and will grind a full hopper of wheat (3lb./1.3kg) in about nine minutes. There is a choice of five settings: 5 being the coarsest and 1 being the finest setting. Setting 5 is more suitable for a coarse-textured bread. The flour from wheat passed through setting 1 twice produces flour that is ideal for short-crust pastry and cakes. Setting 3 produces a flour of a grade halfway between 1 and 5. The Kenwood Wheat Mill is also suitable for grinding other oil-free grains similar in size to wheat such as lentils, barley, rice, millet and buckwheat.

Cooking with Kenwood wholemeal flour
For many recipes you can use the flour just as it comes through the mill. This is surely the best flour to use as none of the nutritional value of the grain is lost. It also provides the natural roughage which is so important in our diet (and is non-existent in many of the over-processed foods we eat today).

When you introduce home-milled flour into your cooking you will find it feels and 'handles' rather differently from commercially produced flour. As you will be using all – or at least a high proportion – of the bran, the amount of rising that takes place during cooking will be less. With home-milled flour you will find that the texture is closer than it would be if the same dish were made with commercially milled white flour.

Storing wheat
Unmilled wheat will keep for about twelve months if stored correctly. Grain should be stored in clean, dry, sealed containers and kept in a cool, dry, airy place which should also be pest and rodent free. Small quantities of grain may be stored in sealed polythene bags in the bottom of a refrigerator.

Weights and measures
The recipes in this book have been written to give successful results whether you choose to use the Imperial measures (left hand column) or the Metric measures (right hand column). Keep to one column or the other. Do not try to make comparisons between the two columns because they are not exact conversions.

Imperial Weight	Exact Conversion	Metric Equivalent Used
½oz.	14.2g	15g
1oz.	28.35g	25g
4oz.	113.4g	100g
8oz.	226.8g	200g
1lb.	453.6g	400g
2lb.	907.2g	1 kg
Liquid		
1fl.oz.	28.35ml	25ml
5fl.oz.	141.75ml	125ml
1 pint	567ml	500ml or ½ litre
1¾ pints	992.25ml	1 litre
Length		
1 inch	2.54cm	2.5cm
6 inch	15.20cm	15cm

One rounded teaspoon	= 1 × 5ml spoon
One level dessertspoon	= 1 × 15ml spoon
One level tablespoon	= 1 × 20ml spoon

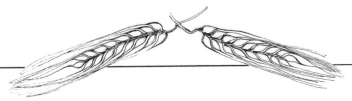

BREAD

BREAD

Cooking with yeast is not the time-consuming, arm-aching chore that is generally supposed. Nowadays more and more people are rolling up their sleeves and making their own bread and yeasted cakes, because there is no doubt that nothing surpasses the flavour and fragrance of home-made breads.

Using a Kenwood Chef mixer with a dough hook attachment will make dough-making even simpler. Time spent kneading dough by hand – around ten to fifteen minutes – can be reduced to about two minutes, speeding up the whole operation considerably. It is now possible for people to make up a week's supply of bread at one time, bake it, freeze it, and thaw it when required. A Chef, dough hook, and wheatmill are the ideal combination for the home baker.

Choice of ingredients

The basic ingredients for bread are flour, yeast, salt and liquid. These ingredients remain fairly inexpensive in relation to others, helping bread to play its important part in our everyday diet.

Flour

Although ordinary plain flour may be used, the best results are obtained by using a 'strong' plain flour milled from hard wheats having a high proportion of gluten or protein (about 10–15 per cent). This type of flour absorbs more liquid, making an elastic dough to form a loaf with greater volume and lighter texture. Strong plain flour is now widely available from most large supermarket chains and health food shops, and is normally a little more expensive than ordinary plain flour. Softer flours, with a protein content of 7–10 per cent, will produce loaves with a closer texture and limited rise. Brown or wholemeal flours give variety in colour and flavour to bread. The high proportion of wheatgerm and bran present in the flour has a softening effect on the protein, and bread baked with these flours will have a closer, 'nutty' texture. The finished result will vary according to the brand of flour used. If you prefer a lighter brown loaf, use half wholemeal and half white flour.

If milling your own flour with the Kenwood wheatmill you can use the flour as it comes from the mill.

Yeast

Yeast is a living organism. Originally it was taken from the surface of beer and wine and in days gone by it was sold by brewers to the farmers' wives on market day. The women carried it home in earthenware pots covered with cloths.

Dried yeast was first prepared for use during long sea voyages. A thin layer of fresh yeast was spread out on a board to dry, then covered with another layer which was allowed to dry and covered with more. The process was repeated until the dried yeast was about two inches thick. It was then cut into squares, prised off the board and stored.

Nowadays the yeast used for bread-making is prepared from molasses or from malted grain, or as a by-product of distilling. It may be bought in cake form 'fresh' or granular form 'dried'. Fresh yeast is normally bought from bakers, whereas dried yeast is available from supermarkets, health food shops and chemists. Brewer's yeast, tonic yeast, and autolysed yeast are not suitable for use in home baking.

Fresh yeast wrapped in polythene or foil will keep two to three days in a cold place, four to five days in a refrigerator, and up to one month in a freezer.

Dried yeast will keep for up to six months if stored in an airtight tin in a cool place.

Yeast quantities will vary according to the type of dough. The standard quantity for plain bread is 1oz./25g yeast to every 2lb./800g flour. Ingredients such as wholemeal flour, eggs, sugar, fruit and larger quantities of fat retard the growth of yeast, making additional yeast necessary in recipes including them.

A given quantity of dried yeast is equivalent to double the quantity of fresh yeast. For example, if 1oz./25g fresh yeast is called for, use ½oz./15g dried yeast. Dried yeast will produce the same results as fresh yeast if the instructions are carefully followed. Yeast works by releasing carbon dioxide which leavens the dough, giving bread its characteristic scent and texture. To do this it requires warm liquid (110°F/43°C), sugar – normally available in the flour – and time. Warmth speeds up the working of the yeast, but excessive heat kills it.

Liquid

The liquid used may be water or milk or a mixture of both. Sometimes fruit juice is used; this has the advantage of a high acid content which strengthens the gluten. Milk makes bread more nutritious, softens the crust and improves its keeping qualities. However, it should be scalded and cooled before use or the lactic acid present may have a detrimental effect on the dough. The basic proportion is 1 pint/500ml liquid to 2lb./800g flour. Soft flours will absorb slightly less liquid.

Different batches of flour vary slightly in their rate of water absorbancy and so it may be necessary to add a little extra flour or more water to get a smooth elastic dough.

Salt

Salt is important for flavour. However, too much will kill the yeast, and exclusion will result in a poor sticky dough, as salt helps to strengthen the gluten.

Sugar

Sugar is a food for yeast. There is normally sufficient present in the flour itself, although a small quantity of sugar, about 1 tsp./5ml is necessary in the reconstitution of dried yeast. Fresh yeast should never be creamed with sugar, as such a high concentration has the effect of killing the yeast cells, giving rise to the yeasty flavour sometimes associated with home-made bread.

Fat

Butter, margarine or lard may be used to enrich the dough. Crumb structure and colour will be improved together with keeping qualities and loaf volume.

Eggs

Eggs enrich the dough and increase its food value.

Other ingredients

As you will see in the recipe section, many different ingredients may be added to the dough. These include dried fruits, nuts, herbs, spices, malt and cheese. Yeasted mixtures are, therefore, really extremely versatile.

Dried fruit should be warmed before it is added to the dough or it will slow the rising. Malt has the effect of softening gluten, and this is why malt breads always have a soft sticky texture.

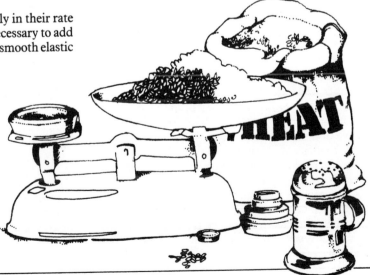

Vitamin C

Vitamin C, or ascorbic acid, is used in the 'short-time' method of bread-making. This reduces the total preparation time by cutting the first rise to 5–10 minutes. The dough may then be shaped and left to rise for the second time. For more details see page 116.

BREAD-MAKING

For all yeast recipes there are three ways of adding yeast to the flour.

1. **Dissolved Yeast Method**

   This method is suitable for most yeasted recipes.

   Fresh yeast: Crumble the fresh yeast into the liquid. Blend with a spoon and add to the flour to form a dough.

   Dried yeast: dissolve 1 tsp./5ml sugar in the warm (110°F/43°C) liquid. Sprinkle the dried yeast on the top. Leave in a warm place until frothy – 10–20 minutes – then add to dry ingredients to form a dough.

2. **Sponge Batter Method**

   This method is more generally used for rich yeast recipes. Fresh or dried yeast may be used.
   Make a batter with:
   ⅓ of the flour in the recipe
   the yeast, fresh or dried
   the liquid, warmed
   1 tsp./5ml sugar
   Do not add the salt at this stage. The batter should be mixed, covered and left in a warm place for about 20 minutes until it froths up and resembles a sponge. In fact this is sometimes known as 'spongeing'. Add the remainder of the ingredients and mix to a firm dough.

3. **Rubbing-in Method**

   This method is suitable for fresh yeast only. Rub the yeast into the flour – it does not have to be very thoroughly mixed – add the liquid and knead well to distribute the yeast.

Mixing the dough

By hand: make a well in the centre of the dry ingredients. Add all the liquid and beat until the mixture is smooth and leaves the sides of the bowl clean. Some people find it easier to do this by hand, but you can use a wooden spoon, spatula or fork.

By machine: place the yeast and liquid into the mixer bowl. Add the dry ingredients. Mix, using a dough hook on the minimum speed, until all the ingredients have been incorporated. Take care to read the manufacturer's instructions regarding the maximum quantity of dough which can be accommodated.

Kneading

Yeast doughs must be kneaded after mixing to develop the gluten and make a good dough. The dough will change visibly from a rough looking mass to a smooth elastic dough. This is important for a good rise and crumb structure.

By hand: find a flat surface and using as little flour as possible (too much flour alters the structure of the recipe) form the dough into a ball. Fold over towards you and push down and away with the heel of the hand, turn through 90 degrees and repeat kneading, developing a rocking rhythm. Continue kneading for 10–15 minutes until the dough feels smooth and elastic and leaves your hands clean.

By machine: after mixing, increase the speed very slightly and knead with the dough hook for 1–1½ minutes until the dough is smooth and elastic. If left too long the dough will become over-kneaded. When this happens the dough becomes very wet and sticky looking.

Rising the dough

All yeast doughs must be risen at least once before baking to allow time for the yeast to work. The dough must be covered during this stage to prevent loss of heat and the formation of a skin. Unshaped doughs can be left in the mixing bowl and placed in a large polythene bag or covered with a damp teacloth. Dough can also be placed directly into a large oiled polythene bag tied loosely at the top, a greased, covered plastic container, or a greased saucepan and lid.

When risen adequately the dough will have doubled in size and will spring back when pressed lightly with a floured finger. The time will vary according to the temperature of the room and the type of dough. It may take 45–60 minutes in a warm place, e.g. an airing cupboard, near a fire (not too near or the yeast will be killed); 2 hours at average room temperature; 12 hours in a cold room or larder; 12–14 hours in a refrigerator. Cool or overnight rising is a good idea because it saves waiting around and strengthens the gluten over a longer period of time, making a good textured loaf.

If bread is risen in the refrigerator, return it to room temperature before re-kneading. If the dough has over-risen and collapsed, re-knead it and put it to rise again.

Second kneading or 'knocking back'

The risen dough must be 'knocked back' to distribute the pockets of air and give the loaf an even texture.

By hand: flatten the dough with the knuckles and knead as before until the dough is firm again. This takes about 1–2 minutes.

available from supermarkets, health food shops and chemists. Brewer's yeast, tonic yeast, and autolysed yeast are not suitable for use in home baking.

Fresh yeast wrapped in polythene or foil will keep two to three days in a cold place, four to five days in a refrigerator, and up to one month in a freezer.

Dried yeast will keep for up to six months if stored in an airtight tin in a cool place.

Yeast quantities will vary according to the type of dough. The standard quantity for plain bread is 1oz./25g yeast to every 2lb./800g flour. Ingredients such as wholemeal flour, eggs, sugar, fruit and larger quantities of fat retard the growth of yeast, making additional yeast necessary in recipes including them.

A given quantity of dried yeast is equivalent to double the quantity of fresh yeast. For example, if 1oz./25g fresh yeast is called for, use ½oz./15g dried yeast. Dried yeast will produce the same results as fresh yeast if the instructions are carefully followed. Yeast works by releasing carbon dioxide which leavens the dough, giving bread its characteristic scent and texture. To do this it requires warm liquid (110°F/43°C), sugar – normally available in the flour – and time. Warmth speeds up the working of the yeast, but excessive heat kills it.

Liquid
The liquid used may be water or milk or a mixture of both. Sometimes fruit juice is used; this has the advantage of a high acid content which strengthens the gluten. Milk makes bread more nutritious, softens the crust and improves its keeping qualities. However, it should be scalded and cooled before use or the lactic acid present may have a detrimental effect on the dough. The basic proportion is 1 pint/500ml liquid to 2lb./800g flour. Soft flours will absorb slightly less liquid.

Different batches of flour vary slightly in their rate of water absorbancy and so it may be necessary to add a little extra flour or more water to get a smooth elastic dough.

Salt
Salt is important for flavour. However, too much will kill the yeast, and exclusion will result in a poor sticky dough, as salt helps to strengthen the gluten.

Sugar
Sugar is a food for yeast. There is normally sufficient present in the flour itself, although a small quantity of sugar, about 1 tsp./5ml is necessary in the reconstitution of dried yeast. Fresh yeast should never be creamed with sugar, as such a high concentration has the effect of killing the yeast cells, giving rise to the yeasty flavour sometimes associated with home-made bread.

Fat
Butter, margarine or lard may be used to enrich the dough. Crumb structure and colour will be improved together with keeping qualities and loaf volume.

Eggs
Eggs enrich the dough and increase its food value.

Other ingredients
As you will see in the recipe section, many different ingredients may be added to the dough. These include dried fruits, nuts, herbs, spices, malt and cheese. Yeasted mixtures are, therefore, really extremely versatile.

Dried fruit should be warmed before it is added to the dough or it will slow the rising. Malt has the effect of softening gluten, and this is why malt breads always have a soft sticky texture.

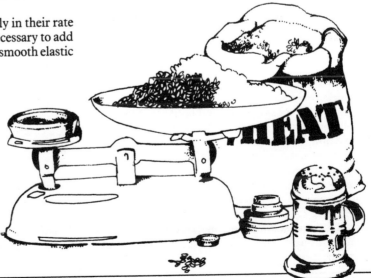

Vitamin C

Vitamin C, or ascorbic acid, is used in the 'short-time' method of bread-making. This reduces the total preparation time by cutting the first rise to 5–10 minutes. The dough may then be shaped and left to rise for the second time. For more details see page 116.

BREAD-MAKING

For all yeast recipes there are three ways of adding yeast to the flour.

1. Dissolved Yeast Method

This method is suitable for most yeasted recipes.

Fresh yeast: Crumble the fresh yeast into the liquid. Blend with a spoon and add to the flour to form a dough.

Dried yeast: dissolve 1 tsp./5ml sugar in the warm (110°F/43°C) liquid. Sprinkle the dried yeast on the top. Leave in a warm place until frothy – 10–20 minutes – then add to dry ingredients to form a dough.

2. Sponge Batter Method

This method is more generally used for rich yeast recipes. Fresh or dried yeast may be used.

Make a batter with:

⅓ of the flour in the recipe

the yeast, fresh or dried

the liquid, warmed

1 tsp./5ml sugar

Do not add the salt at this stage. The batter should be mixed, covered and left in a warm place for about 20 minutes until it froths up and resembles a sponge. In fact this is sometimes known as 'spongeing'. Add the remainder of the ingredients and mix to a firm dough.

3. Rubbing-in Method

This method is suitable for fresh yeast only. Rub the yeast into the flour – it does not have to be very thoroughly mixed – add the liquid and knead well to distribute the yeast.

Mixing the dough

By hand: make a well in the centre of the dry ingredients. Add all the liquid and beat until the mixture is smooth and leaves the sides of the bowl clean. Some people find it easier to do this by hand, but you can use a wooden spoon, spatula or fork.

By machine: place the yeast and liquid into the mixer bowl. Add the dry ingredients. Mix, using a dough hook on the minimum speed, until all the ingredients have been incorporated. Take care to read the manufacturer's instructions regarding the maximum quantity of dough which can be accommodated.

Kneading

Yeast doughs must be kneaded after mixing to develop the gluten and make a good dough. The dough will change visibly from a rough looking mass to a smooth elastic dough. This is important for a good rise and crumb structure.

By hand: find a flat surface and using as little flour as possible (too much flour alters the structure of the recipe) form the dough into a ball. Fold over towards you and push down and away with the heel of the hand, turn through 90 degrees and repeat kneading, developing a rocking rhythm. Continue kneading for 10–15 minutes until the dough feels smooth and elastic and leaves your hands clean.

By machine: after mixing, increase the speed very slightly and knead with the dough hook for 1–1½ minutes until the dough is smooth and elastic. If left too long the dough will become over-kneaded. When this happens the dough becomes very wet and sticky looking.

Rising the dough

All yeast doughs must be risen at least once before baking to allow time for the yeast to work. The dough must be covered during this stage to prevent loss of heat and the formation of a skin. Unshaped doughs can be left in the mixing bowl and placed in a large polythene bag or covered with a damp teacloth. Dough can also be placed directly into a large oiled polythene bag tied loosely at the top, a greased, covered plastic container, or a greased saucepan and lid.

When risen adequately the dough will have doubled in size and will spring back when pressed lightly with a floured finger. The time will vary according to the temperature of the room and the type of dough. It may take 45–60 minutes in a warm place, e.g. an airing cupboard, near a fire (not too near or the yeast will be killed); 2 hours at average room temperature; 12 hours in a cold room or larder; 12–14 hours in a refrigerator. Cool or overnight rising is a good idea because it saves waiting around and strengthens the gluten over a longer period of time, making a good textured loaf.

If bread is risen in the refrigerator, return it to room temperature before re-kneading. If the dough has over-risen and collapsed, re-knead it and put it to rise again.

Second kneading or 'knocking back'

The risen dough must be 'knocked back' to distribute the pockets of air and give the loaf an even texture.

By hand: flatten the dough with the knuckles and knead as before until the dough is firm again. This takes about 1–2 minutes.

By machine: knead using the machine and dough hook using a low speed for ½–1 minute until the dough is firm again.

Shaping

The dough is now ready for shaping to fit tins or to make freehand shapes such as plaits, buns, or cottage loaves. Take care not to use too much flour during shaping as this will spoil the colour of the loaf. The finished loaf should be smooth, and any joins or ends must be tucked away underneath.

Tin loaves

Divide the dough into 1lb./400g pieces approximately. Stretch each piece into an oblong as wide as the length of the tins. Fold into three and turn over so that the seam is underneath. Smooth over the top, tuck in the ends and place in greased 1lb. loaf tins. Prove and bake at 450°F/230°C/Gas Mark 8 for 30–35 minutes.

Rolls

Divide the dough into 2oz./50g pieces. Roll each piece into a ball using the palm of the hand. This is best done on an unfloured board with a little flour in the palm of the hand. Place rolls on lightly greased trays and prove. Brush with egg or milk. Bake near the top of the oven at 450°F/230°C/Gas Mark 8 for 15–20 minutes.

Poppy seed plaits

Divide the dough into 1lb./400g pieces approximately. Cut each piece into three, roll each third into a long thin sausage, and place side by side. Gather the three ends together and form a plait, tucking the ends underneath to neaten. After proving on a. baking sheet, brush with beaten egg or milk and sprinkle with poppy seeds. Bake at 450°F/230°C/Gas Mark 8 for 30–35 minutes.

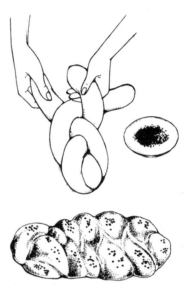

Crown loaf

1½lbs./600g flour makes two crown loaves.

Divide the dough in half. Divide each half into six equal pieces. Roll each piece into a smooth ball (see bread rolls). Place in greased 6 inch/15cm sandwich tins using five to form a ring with the sixth in the centre. Leave to prove. Brush with egg wash and sprinkle with poppy seeds. Bake just above the centre of a hot oven at 450°F/230°C/Gas Mark 8 for 25–30 minutes.

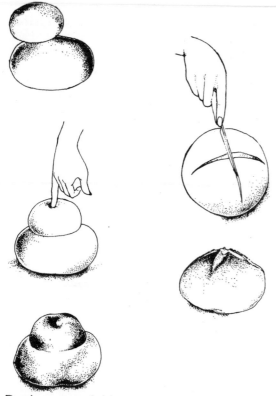

450°F/230°C/Gas Mark 8. You may find that the recommended temperature varies slightly from recipe to recipe. Enriched breads are cooked at slightly lower temperatures: 375°–425°F/190°–220°C/Gas Mark 5–7.

When cooked, the loaves will shrink away from sides of the tin and will sound hollow when the bottoms are tapped with the knuckles. The crust should be a deep golden brown.

Cool on a wire rack to prevent steam softening the crust.

WHAT WENT WRONG?

Do remember that bread-making, like other more specialized areas of cookery, is a skill; something that is improved each time it is practised. If you have a failure, don't despair, cast your eye over the list below, pinpoint the fault, and try again.

Poor volume, pale crust and flat top
The dough was either too wet or too dry.
There was not enough salt or yeast.
The flour was too soft.
The proving temperature was too high and/or too long.
The dough was insufficiently kneaded or under-risen.

'Flying top' or cracked crust
The flour was too soft.
There was insufficient rising and proving.
Too much dough for the size of tin.

Heavy close texture
The flour was too soft.
There was too much salt.
There was insufficient kneading.
The rising time was too short.
The yeast may have been killed by rising in too hot a place.
The oven was too cool, making the total baking time excessive.

Uneven texture and holes
Too much liquid or salt.
Insufficient or excessive rising time.
Insufficiently kneaded after the first rising.
The dough was over-proved.
The dough was left uncovered during rising, thereby forming a skin, which led to streaks when re-kneaded.

Proving or second rising
Dough has to be proved in order to regain volume lost during the second kneading and shaping. Place tins inside a large oiled polythene bag tied loosely. Leave in a warm – not hot – place until the dough is doubled in size and springs back when pressed lightly with a floured finger.

Finishes
Finish loaves in one of the following ways.

Before baking, brush tops with egg wash (1 egg, 1 tsp./5ml sugar and 1 tbsp./20ml water beaten together); lightly salted water, or milk, or dust with flour or just leave plain. Some breads are sprinkled with poppy seeds, sesame seeds, cheese or cracked wheat. (Sesame seeds, poppy seeds, and cracked wheat can be bought from health food shops.) Sweet breads are often brushed with clear honey, sugar glaze (1 tbsp./20ml caster sugar and 2 tbsp./40ml water heated till sugar dissolves) or coated with sugar and water icing after baking. Or, you can brush loaves with butter when you take them out of the oven.

Baking
Before baking remove any covering used during proving. Bake wholemeal and white bread at

Sour acid and yeasty flavour
Too much yeast.
Stale yeast.
Yeast creamed with sugar.
Excessive rising time.

Bread stales quickly and is crumbly
Too much yeast.
The flour was too soft.
Too much fat.
The dough was over-risen.

Staling

In spite of what many people think, staling is not just bread drying out.

Staling is divided into two kinds: crust staling, and crumb staling. Crust staling appears to be caused by transfer of moisture from the crumb to the crust, causing it to go soft. Crumb staling is more of a mystery, and is generally supposed to be caused by a chemical process.

Storage of bread

Some breads will keep better than others. Enriched breads, starch-reduced breads, and sliced breads, will generally keep fresh for several days if stored correctly, whilst an authentic French 'baguette' will only keep fresh for a matter of hours.

Bread should be stored at room temperature in a clean, dry, well ventilated container. Air should be allowed to circulate around the bread in order to keep the crust crisp. The container should be kept free of crumbs, washed each week and dried carefully. Wrapped bread should be kept in its own wrapper.

Freezing bread

Both home-made and bought bread can be stored in the freezer. Wrap the bread in foil or polythene and seal tightly before freezing. It will keep for about three months. To thaw, stand the wrapped bread at room temperature for 4–6 hours. Crusty loaves will need to be crisped in a hot oven for about 10 minutes. Slices of cut bread can be toasted straight from the freezer.

Notes for owners of microwave ovens

Dough can be risen in a microwave oven. A 1lb./400g batch of dough will take 20–25 minutes. In this time the dough will double in size quickly and evenly. Place the kneaded dough in a bowl covered with cling film, put in your microwave oven and give 15 second bursts, followed by rest intervals of 5 minutes. Time the bursts of energy carefully – too much may kill the yeast. Soft crusted rolls and bread may be cooked in a microwave oven, but this method is unsuitable if a golden and/or crisp crust is required. It is difficult to be precise about cooking time, as much depends upon the model of oven. Refer to your instruction manual for guidance.

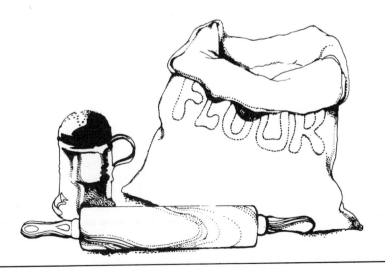

WHITE BREAD

Standard method

1½ pints/750ml warm
   water
1oz./25g fresh yeast *or*
   ½oz./15g dried yeast
   plus 1 tsp./5ml caster
   sugar
3lb./1.5kg strong plain
   flour
3 tsp./15ml salt
1oz./25g lard

Pour the liquid into a bowl, crumble in the fresh yeast *or* stir in the sugar and sprinkle the dried yeast on top and leave for about 15 minutes or until frothy. Sift the flour and salt together. If mixing by hand rub the fat into the sifted flour and salt. Make a well in the centre of the flour, add the yeast liquid and mix to form a soft dough. If using a mixer, add the yeast mixture to the flour with the fat in one piece. Mix on a low speed until a soft dough is formed.

Knead the dough until smooth and elastic. This will take 10–15 minutes by hand or 1–2 minutes in a mixer. Place the bowl inside a lightly oiled polythene bag or cover with a damp cloth and leave in a warm place for 45–60 minutes or until dough has doubled in size.

Re-knead until smooth and shape as required (see page 15). Place the shaped dough in an oiled polythene bag or cover with a damp cloth and leave in a warm place for ½ hour or until doubled in bulk.

Bake at 450°F/230°C/Gas Mark 8, for 30–35 minutes for loaves, or for 15–20 minutes for rolls, or until well risen and golden brown. Cool on a wire rack.
Makes four 1lb. loaves or 36 rolls.

NOTE: In all subsequent recipes which refer to the method for Standard White Bread, add the fat as instructed above unless the recipe specifies otherwise.

The 'short time' method of bread-making
The 'short time' method of bread-making enables you to make bread in approximately 1¾ hours. It is suitable for both plain breads and enriched doughs. However, only fresh yeast should be used, as the time taken to reconstitute dried yeast defeats the advantage of this method.

This method relies on the addition of a small amount of Vitamin C (ascorbic acid) which reduces the time of the first rising to 5 minutes for plain doughs or 10 minutes for enriched doughs. To ensure the success of this type of recipe, extra yeast and additional sugar are used. Use liquid 90–95°F/32–35°C if your kitchen is cool, or 80–85°F/27–30°C if it is warm to be sure of successful results.

QUICK WHITE BREAD

1½ tsp./7.5ml sugar
¾ pint/375ml warm water
1oz./25g fresh yeast
25mg ascorbic acid
1½lb./600g strong plain
   flour
2 tsp./10ml salt
½oz./15g lard

Dissolve the sugar in the warm water and crumble in the fresh yeast and ascorbic acid. Sift the flour and salt together. If mixing by hand rub the lard into the flour. Make a well in the centre of the flour and add the yeast liquid and mix to form a soft dough. If using a mixer, add the flour and lard to the yeast liquid and mix on a low speed until a soft dough is formed.

Knead the dough until smooth and elastic. This will take about 10 minutes by hand or 1–2 minutes in a mixer.

Place the bowl inside a lightly greased polythene bag and leave to stand for 5 minutes. Re-knead for 2 or 3 minutes by hand or 1 minute in a mixer. Shape the dough into loaves or rolls as required. Place the tins or baking trays inside a large, lightly greased polythene bag and leave to rise for 45–50 minutes in a warm place. Bake at 450°F/230°C/Gas Mark 8 for 40–45 minutes or until well-risen or golden brown.

QUICK WHOLEMEAL BREAD

This recipe has a lighter texture than ordinary wholemeal bread, as it is made with half white and half wholemeal flour; if you wish you can use all wholemeal flour.

¾ pint/375ml warm water
1oz./25g fresh yeast *or*
   ½oz./15g dried yeast
   plus 1 level tsp./5ml
   sugar
12oz./350g wholemeal
   flour
12oz./350g strong white
   flour
2 level tsp./10ml salt
crushed wheat or
   cornflakes to decorate

Pour the water into a bowl, crumble in the fresh yeast *or* stir in the sugar and sprinkle the dried yeast on top. Leave for about 15 minutes until frothy. Sift the flour and salt into a mixing bowl. Make a well in the centre of the flour, add the yeast liquid, and mix to form a soft dough.

Knead until the dough is smooth and elastic. This will take about 10 minutes by hand or 1–2 minutes in a mixer. The dough is now ready for shaping into three loaves. Brush the tops with salt water and sprinkle with lightly crushed cornflakes or crushed wheat. Place the shaped loaves in an oiled polythene bag or cover with a damp cloth and leave in a warm place for 1½ hours or until doubled in bulk. The dough is ready to cook when it springs back when pressed lightly with a floured finger.

Bake at 450°F/230°C/Gas Mark 8 for 30–40 minutes. Cool on a wire rack.
Makes three 1lb. loaves.

FLOWERPOT LOAVES

1 batch of Quick
   Wholemeal Bread (see
   above)

To prepare new flowerpots
Grease the earthenware flowerpots well and bake empty in a hot oven. Repeat the process several times. This will prevent the loaves from sticking and for further use simply grease the flower pots in the normal way as for baking tins.

After the first kneading, divide dough into three and shape each piece to fit a 5 inch/13cm diameter well-greased earthenware flowerpot.

Put the dough to rise inside a large, well-greased polythene bag and leave until the dough has doubled in size and springs back when pressed lightly with a floured finger. Brush tops with salt water and sprinkle with lightly crushed cornflakes or crushed wheat.

Bake at 450°F/230°C/Gas Mark 8 for 20–30 minutes. Cool on a wire rack.

BRIDGE ROLLS

½oz./15g fresh yeast or
2 tsp./10ml dried yeast
   plus ½ tsp./2.5ml caster
   sugar
7fl.oz./175ml warm milk
12oz./300g strong plain
   flour
1 tsp./5ml salt
½oz./15g lard
beaten egg to glaze

Follow the method for white bread (see page 18) until the dough has been kneaded for the first time. Divide dough into 30 pieces, and shape each into finger rolls approximately 3 inches/7.5cm in length. Arrange the rolls on a greased baking sheet close together but not touching. Allow to prove until the rolls have risen and touch each other. Brush with beaten egg and bake at 425°F/220°C/Gas Mark 7 for 15 minutes. Cool on a wire rack.
Makes approximately 30 rolls.

A RICHER RECIPE FOR BRIDGE ROLLS

½oz./15g fresh yeast *or*
  2 tsp./10ml dried yeast
  plus ½ tsp./2.5ml caster
  sugar
½ pint/250ml warm milk
1lb./400g strong plain
  flour

1 tsp./5ml salt
4oz./100g butter
1 egg, beaten
beaten egg to glaze

Follow the method for bridge rolls (page 19), rubbing the butter into the flour and adding the beaten egg with the yeast liquid.
Makes approximately 30 rolls.

BAPS

½ pint/250ml warm milk
1oz./25g fresh yeast *or*
  1 tbsp./20ml dried yeast
  plus 1 tsp./5ml caster
  sugar

1lb./400g ordinary plain
  flour
1 tsp./5ml salt
2oz./50g lard, rubbed in

Follow the method for white bread (see page 18) until the dough has been kneaded and risen for the first time. Divide the dough into eight equal pieces, shape into balls and flatten the tops with the palm of the hand. Place on a greased baking sheet and leave to rise again.

  Gently pat the tops of the baps to flatten slightly after they have proved. Dust with flour, bake at 450°F/230°C/Gas Mark 8 for 10–15 minutes. Cool on a wire rack.
Makes 8 baps.

WHOLEMEAL SCONE LOAF

This bread is best eaten on the day it is made.

½oz./15g fresh yeast *or*
  2 tsp./10ml dried yeast
  plus 1 tsp./5ml caster
  sugar
½ pint/250ml warm water

4 tbsp./80ml double or
  clotted cream
1lb./400g wholemeal flour
1 tsp./5ml salt

Follow the method for white bread (see page 18), adding the cream to the yeast liquid. Proceed until the dough has been kneaded and risen once. Shape dough into a ball, flatten the top slightly and place onto a greased baking sheet. Make 4–6 deep cuts across the top and leave to rise a second time. Bake at 425°F/220°C/Gas Mark 7 for approximately 45 minutes. Cool on a wire rack.

KENTISH HUFKINS

½oz./15g fresh yeast *or*
  2 tsp./10ml dried yeast
  plus 1 tsp./5ml caster
  sugar
½ pint/250ml warm milk
  and water

1lb./400g strong white
  flour
½ tsp./2.5ml salt
1oz./25g lard, rubbed in

Follow the method for white bread (see page 18) until the dough has been kneaded and risen for the first time. Divide the dough into 10 pieces. Roll each piece into a ball and flatten with a rolling pin to form a flat oval cake, about ½ inch/12mm thick. Place on a greased baking sheet well apart and press a floured finger into the centre of each cake. Allow to rise again, then bake at 450°F/230°C/Gas Mark 8 for 15–20 minutes. Cool on a wire rack. Serve buttered, hot or cold.
Makes 10 hufkins.

DEVONSHIRE SPLITS

2oz./50g butter
2oz./50g caster sugar
½ pint/250ml warm milk
½oz./15g fresh yeast *or*
  2 tsp./10ml dried yeast
  plus 1 tsp./5ml caster
  sugar
1lb./400g strong plain
  flour
1 tsp./5ml salt

Filling
6–8 tbsp./120–160ml red
  jam
½ pint/250ml double or
  clotted cream
icing sugar to dredge

Melt the butter and sugar in the warm milk, and proceed as for white bread (see page 18) frothing the yeast in the milk mixture. After the first rise divide the dough into 14–16 pieces. Roll each piece into a ball and place on a greased baking sheet. Flatten the tops slightly, leave to rise again and bake at 425°F/220°C/Gas Mark 7 for 15–20 minutes. Cool on a wire rack. To serve, split and spread with jam and cream and dust tops with icing sugar.
Makes 14–16 splits.

SALLY LUNN

This teacake is said to be called after Sally Lunn, who had a pastry-cook's shop in Bath during the 18th century.

2oz./50g butter
2 tsp./10ml caster sugar
½ pint/250ml milk
½oz./15g fresh yeast *or*
  2 tsp./10ml dried yeast
1lb./400g strong plain
  flour
1 tsp./5ml salt
2 eggs, beaten

Sugar glaze
1 tbsp./20ml sugar
1 tbsp./20ml water

Dissolve the butter and sugar in the warm milk. Add the yeast to the warm liquid. Leave for a few minutes until the yeast begins to work. Sift the flour and the salt together. Make a well in the centre of the dry ingredients and pour in the yeast liquid and the beaten eggs. Beat well to form a soft dough. (It will be too soft to knead.) Place into two greased 5 inch/12.5cm cake tins. Cover and leave in a warm place to prove for about 1½ hours. Bake in a hot oven at 425°F/220°C/Gas Mark 7 for 20–25 minutes. Turn out onto a wire rack.

Prepare the glaze by boiling the sugar and water together for 2 minutes. Brush the tops of the teacakes with the sugar glaze while still hot. Serve filled with butter or cream.
Makes 2 teacakes.

MILK LOAF

This loaf is nicest eaten on the day it is made.

1lb./400g ordinary plain
  flour
½oz./15g fresh yeast *or*
  2 tsp./10ml dried yeast
  plus 1 tsp./5ml caster
  sugar

8fl.oz./200ml warm milk
1 tsp./5ml salt
2oz./50g butter
1 egg, beaten

Place one third of the flour in a bowl, and add sugar, yeast and milk. Mix well and leave in a warm place until frothy. Rub the butter into the remaining flour, sifted with the salt. Add the egg and yeast mixture to the flour and beat well. Knead until the dough loses its stickiness. Cover and leave to rise in a warm place for 1 hour or until doubled in size. Re-knead and shape to fit a greased 1lb. loaf tin. Cover and leave to rise in a warm place until dough reaches top of the tin. Brush the top with milk, bake at 375°F/190°C/Gas Mark 5 for 45–50 minutes, or until golden brown. Cool on a wire rack.

MANCHETS

Manchet is the name given to a fairly small loaf made of the 'finest wheaten flour'. Manchets have been made since the 15th century and were the forerunners of the softer, light doughs that we know today.

½oz./15g fresh yeast *or*
  2 tsp./10ml dried yeast
  plus 1 tsp./5ml caster
  sugar
12½fl.oz./315ml warm
  milk and water

1½oz./40g butter
10oz./250g strong white
  flour
10oz./250g wholemeal
  flour

Froth the dried yeast with the sugar in the warm water and milk *or* crumble the fresh yeast in the liquid. Sieve the flours and the salt into a bowl and rub in the butter and add the yeast liquid. Knead to form the dough, cover and leave in a warm place to rise until doubled in bulk. Re-knead, divide into four and form into bun shapes. Place on greased baking trays. Cover and leave to rise again until doubled in bulk. Make a deep cut down the centre of each manchet and put immediately into the oven. Bake at 425°F/220°C/Gas Mark 7 for approximately 30 minutes. Cool on a wire rack.

PLANK BREAD

Traditionally this bread should be cooked on a plank; however, nowadays a greased cast iron frying pan is more practical.

½oz./15g fresh yeast *or*
  2 tsp./10ml dried yeast
  plus 1 tsp./5ml sugar
½ pint/250ml warm milk
  and water

1lb./400g strong plain
  flour
1oz./25g lard
½ tsp./2.5ml salt

Froth dried yeast with sugar in the warm liquid *or* crumble fresh yeast into the warm liquid. Rub lard into the flour, add the salt. Make a well in the centre and add the yeast liquid and knead. Cover and leave to rise in a warm place for 1 hour or until almost doubled in bulk. Divide into four, knead and roll out into circles approximately ¼–½ inch/6–12mm thick. Cover and leave to rise for 10–15 minutes. Lightly grease a heavy-based frying pan and cook the bread over a low heat for 15–20 minutes on each side.
  Serve hot or cold, split and buttered.

BREAD STICKS

½oz./15g fresh yeast *or*
  2 tsp./10ml dried yeast
  plus ½ tsp./2.5ml sugar
7fl.oz./175ml warm milk

12oz./300g strong plain
  flour
1 level tsp./5ml salt

Froth the dried yeast and sugar into the warm milk *or* crumble the fresh yeast into the warm milk. Sift flour and salt together and add yeast liquid. Knead until smooth and elastic. Cover the bowl and leave in a warm place to rise. Re-knead the dough, and divide into 24 pieces. Roll pieces into even lengths, the thickness of a pencil. Place on greased baking trays, cover and leave to prove. Bake at 400°F/200°C/Gas Mark 6 for 15–20 minutes until crisp and they will snap in half. Cool on a wire rack.
Makes approximately 24 sticks.

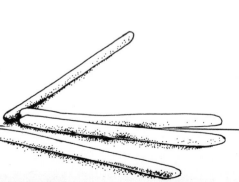

BRAN BREAD

2oz./50g bran
1oz./25g soya flour
1½lb./600g wholemeal
 flour
1½ tsp./7.5ml salt

1oz./25g fresh yeast *or*
 1 tbsp./20ml dried yeast
 plus 1 tsp./5ml caster
 sugar
1 pint/500ml warm water

The bran may be sieved from flour milled in the wheatmill. Add bran and soya flour to the wholemeal flour and salt and follow the method for white bread (see page 18). Knead, cover and leave in a warm place to rise for the first time. Re-knead and shape to fit a 2lb. loaf tin. Cover and leave to prove until double in size. Bake at 400°F/200°C/Gas Mark 6 for 40–50 minutes. Cool on a wire rack.

LIGHT RYE BREAD

½oz./15g fresh yeast *or*
 2 tsp./10ml dried yeast
 plus ½ tsp./2.5ml caster
 sugar
4fl.oz./100ml warm water
½ pint/250ml milk
1 tbsp./20ml black treacle
1oz./25g lard
1lb/400g rye flour
8oz./200g strong plain
 flour

Glaze
1 tsp./5ml cornflour
4 tbsp./80ml cold water
boiling water to mix

Froth the dried yeast with the sugar and warm water *or* crumble the fresh yeast in the water. Heat the milk and black treacle until lukewarm. Rub the lard into the sifted flour and salt. Make a well in the centre of the flour and pour in the yeast and milk mixtures. Draw the flours into the liquid and mix until the dough comes cleanly away from the sides of the bowl. Knead until the dough is smooth and elastic. Cover with a damp cloth and leave to rise in a warm place for 1 hour or until double in bulk. Re-knead, divide into two, and shape either into two round or oblong loaves. Place on a greased baking sheet, cover and prove. Prepare the glaze by mixing the cornflour and cold water together. Heat together in a pan until the mixture thickens and clears. Brush on top of the dough. Bake at 425°F/220°C/Gas Mark 7 for 40–50 minutes. Cool on a wire rack.

OATMEAL RYE BREAD

1oz./25g fresh yeast *or*
 1 tbsp./20ml dried yeast
 plus 1 tsp./5ml caster
 sugar
1 pint/500ml warm milk
 and water
1lb./400g wholemeal flour
1lb./400g ordinary plain
 flour

8oz./200g fine oatmeal
8oz./200g rye flour
2 tsp./10ml salt
1oz./25g molasses
4fl.oz./100ml oil

Froth the dried yeast in the warm milk and water with the sugar *or* crumble the fresh yeast into the liquid. Combine the flours, oatmeal and salt. Make a well in the centre and pour in the yeast mixture, molasses and oil. Draw the flours into the liquid and mix until dough is formed. Knead for 10–15 minutes. This will be a stiff dough. Cover with a damp cloth and leave in a warm place for 1 hour or until doubled in bulk.

Re-knead the dough for 1–2 minutes and shape into two oval loaves. Place the loaves on greased trays, cover with a damp cloth and prove until doubled in size. Bake at 425°F/220°C/Gas Mark 7 for ¾ hour approximately. If desired brush the bread with milk 10 minutes before the end of cooking time. Turn out of the tins and cool on a wire rack.

WHOLEMEAL RICE BREAD

1oz./25g fresh yeast *or*
   1 tbsp./20ml dried yeast
2oz./50g honey
½ pint/250ml warm water
½oz./15g lard

6oz./150g rice flour
2oz./50g soya flour
12oz./300g wholemeal
   flour
1 tsp./5ml salt

Froth the dried yeast in the warm water and honey *or* crumble in the fresh yeast. Leave for 10–15 minutes. Rub the lard into the sifted rice flour, soya flour, wholemeal flour and salt. Make a well in the centre of the dry ingredients and pour in the yeast mixture and mix until a dough is formed. Knead until smooth and elastic. Cover with a damp cloth and leave to rise in a warm place for 1 hour or until doubled in bulk. Re-knead and shape to fit a greased 2lb. loaf tin. Cover and allow to prove. Bake at 400°F/200°C/Gas Mark 6 for 15 minutes. Reduce the temperature to 350°F/180°C/Gas Mark 4 for a further 30 minutes. Remove from tin and cool on a wire rack.

SODA BREAD

This unyeasted bread is traditionally made in Ireland.

1lb./400g ordinary plain
   flour
2 tsp./10ml baking powder
1 tsp./5ml salt

1 tsp./5ml sugar
1oz./25g lard or margarine
½ pint/250ml milk

Sieve flour, baking powder and salt in a bowl, add sugar, rub in fat until the mixture resembles fine breadcrumbs. Make a well in the centre and add the milk to form a soft dough. Knead until smooth. Form into a circle about 7 inches/17.5cm in diameter and place on a greased baking sheet. Mark a fairly deep cross on the top. Bake at 425°F/220°C/Gas Mark 7 for 10 minutes and reduce to 400°F/200°C/Gas Mark 6 and bake for a further 30 minutes. The bread is cooked if the base sounds hollow when tapped. Cool on a wire rack.

CHEESE LOAF

½ pint/250ml warm water
½oz./15g fresh yeast, *or*
   2 tsp./10ml dried yeast
   plus 1 tsp./5ml sugar
1lb./400g strong plain
   flour

2 tsp./10ml salt
1 tsp./5ml dry mustard
pinch of pepper
4–6oz./100–150g Cheddar
   cheese, finely grated

Variation
Cheese and Celery Loaf
Sprinkle an extra 1oz./25g grated cheese mixed with 1 tsp./5ml Celery Salt on top of the loaves before baking.

Pour the liquid into a bowl, crumble on the fresh yeast *or* stir in the sugar, sprinkle the dried yeast on top and leave about 15 minutes until frothy. Make a well in the centre of the flour, add the yeast liquid, mustard, pepper and most of the cheese, and mix to form a soft dough. Knead until the dough is smooth and elastic. This will take 10 minutes by hand or 1–2 minutes in a mixer. Place the bread inside a lightly greased polythene bag and leave to rise until doubled in size. Re-knead until smooth and shape to fit two greased 1lb. loaf tins. Place the tins in a lightly greased polythene bag and prove until the dough reaches the tops of the tins and springs back when pressed with a floured finger. Sprinkle the remaining cheese over the tops of the loaves. Bake at 375°F/190°C/Gas Mark 5 for 45 minutes, or until done. Care should be taken not to overbake. Cool on a wire rack.

ROSEMARY BREAD

This bread can be made either with all wholemeal flour or a mixture of white and wholemeal flour. The amount of dried rosemary used is a matter of personal taste.

White
½oz./15g fresh yeast *or*
   2 tsp./10ml dried yeast plus ½ tsp./2.5ml caster sugar
½ pint/250ml warm water
12oz./300g strong plain flour
4oz./100g wholemeal flour
1 tsp./5ml salt
1 tbsp./20ml dried rosemary

Wholemeal
½oz./15g fresh yeast *or*
   2 tsp./10ml dried yeast plus ½ tsp./2.5ml caster sugar
10–12fl.oz./250–300ml warm water
1lb./400g wholemeal flour
1 tsp./5ml salt
1 tbsp./20ml dried rosemary

Follow the receipe for white bread (see page 18) adding the dried rosemary with the flour. Knead, cover and leave in a warm place to rise for the first time. Re-knead and shape to fit a 2lb. loaf tin. Cover and prove until doubled in size. Brush with milk and sprinkle the top with dried rosemary. Bake at 425°F/220°C/Gas Mark 7 for approximately 35 minutes. Cool on a wire rack.

OAT AND CARAWAY BREAD

10oz./250g wholemeal flour
1 tsp./5ml baking powder
½ tsp./2.5ml bicarbonate of soda
½ tsp./2.5ml salt
1oz./25g butter

3oz./75g rolled oats
1oz./25g wheatgerm
2 tsp./10ml caraway seeds
5fl.oz./125ml sour cream
2 eggs, lightly beaten
3oz./75g soft brown sugar

Sift the flour, baking powder, bicarbonate of soda, and salt into a bowl and rub in the butter. Add the oats, wheatgerm and caraway seeds.

In another bowl, mix the sour cream, eggs and sugar, beating the mixture well. Make a well in the centre of the dry ingredients and pour in the cream mixture. Mix until a soft dough forms.

Turn into a greased 1lb. loaf tin and bake at 350°F/180°C/Gas Mark 4 for 40–45 minutes. Cool on a wire rack.

FRUITY MALT BREAD

8fl.oz./200ml warm water
1oz./25g margarine, softened
2 tbsp./40ml malt extract
1 tbsp./20ml black treacle
1oz./25g fresh yeast *or*
   1 tbsp./20ml dried yeast and 1 tsp./5ml caster sugar

8oz./200g wholewheat flour
8oz./200g plain flour
6oz./150g sultanas
sugar and water to glaze

Pour the liquid into a bowl, add margarine cut into pieces, malt extract, treacle, and yeast. Mix together thoroughly. Add flour and sultanas and combine thoroughly. Knead until the dough is smooth and elastic. Shape into two small loaves (the dough will be very soft to handle). Place on a greased baking sheet, cover and prove until doubled in size. Bake at 400°F/200°C/Gas Mark 6 for 40–45 minutes. Cool on a wire rack and brush with glaze.

BARA BRITH OR WELSH CURRANT BREAD

'Bara' means bread and 'Brith' means currants, sometimes it is known as Welsh Speckled Bread.

1oz./25g fresh yeast *or*
   1 tbsp./20ml dried yeast
   plus 1 tsp./5ml sugar
1lb./400g strong white
   flour
8fl.oz./200ml warm milk
1 tsp./5ml salt
1 tsp./5ml mixed spice
2oz./50g butter
2oz./50g soft brown sugar
10oz./250g mixed dried
   fruit: currants, raisins,
   sultanas, mixed peel
1 egg

Glaze
1oz./25g sugar
2 tbsp./40ml water or milk
   or honey

Mix together sugar, yeast, a quarter of the flour and milk. Cover and set aside in a warm place for about 20 minutes or until frothy. Sift together the remaining flour, salt and spice and rub in the fat. Stir in the brown sugar and dried fruit. Add the flour mixture and egg to the yeast batter and mix well to form a soft dough. Add extra flour if the dough is too sticky. Knead until the dough is smooth and elastic. Cover and leave the dough to rise until doubled in bulk. Re-knead until smooth. Divide into two and shape to fit two 1lb. loaf tins. Prove until the dough stands 1 inch/2.5cm above the top of the tins. Bake at 350°F/180°C/Gas Mark 4, for about 50 minutes. Cool on a wire rack.

Prepare the glaze by dissolving the sugar in the water or milk over a low heat. Bring to the boil, and boil rapidly for 2 minutes. Glaze the tops of the loaves.

BANNOCKS

These are traditionally made in Scotland.

½oz./15g fresh yeast *or*
   2 tsp./10ml dried yeast
   plus 1 tsp./5ml caster
   sugar
½ pint/250ml warm milk
   and water
2oz./50g sugar
1lb./400g plain flour

1 tsp./5ml salt
2oz./50g lard, rubbed into
   flour
1oz./25g sultanas
1oz./25g currants
1oz./25g chopped mixed
   peel

Follow the method for white bread (see page 18), adding the fruit and 2oz./50g sugar with the flour. Knead, cover and leave in a warm place to rise for the first time. Re-knead and form into two round cakes and put onto a greased baking sheet. Cover and allow to prove for 20 minutes. Bake at 350°F/180°C/Gas Mark 4 for 35 minutes until golden brown, turning the loaves once. Cool on a wire rack.

WHOLEMEAL MALT LOAF

1oz./25g fresh yeast *or*
   2 tbsp./20ml dried yeast
   plus 1 tsp./5ml caster
   sugar
½ pint/250ml warm water
1lb./400g wholemeal flour
1 tsp./5ml salt
6oz./150g sultanas
1oz./25g margarine
1 tbsp./20ml black treacle
2 tbsp./40ml malt extract

Glaze
1½oz./40g caster sugar
3fl.oz./75ml milk and
   water

Crumble the fresh yeast into the liquid *or* froth the dried yeast and sugar in the liquid. Mix in the other ingredients and knead well. The dough will be very soft and sticky. Cover and leave in a warm place to rise until doubled in bulk. Re-knead and shape into two small loaves. Place on a greased baking sheet. Cover and prove. Prepare the glaze by dissolving the sugar in the water over a moderate heat, and allow to cool. Brush the loaves with glaze. Bake at 375°F/190°C/Gas Mark 5 for 40–45 minutes. Cool on a wire rack. Serve sliced with butter.

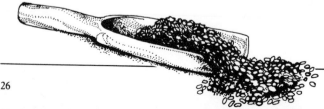

CURRANT BREAD

Use a mixture of 8oz./200g wholemeal flour and 8oz./200g strong plain flour for a more 'nutty' texture.

½oz./15g fresh yeast *or*
  2 tsp./10ml dried yeast
  plus 1 tsp./5ml sugar
1oz./25g caster sugar
½ pint/250ml warm milk
1lb./400g strong plain
  flour
1 tsp./5ml salt
1oz./25g margarine
5oz./125g currants

Glaze
honey

Follow the method for white bread (see page 18), add the currants and 1oz./25g sugar with the flour. Knead, cover and leave in a warm place to rise for the first time. Re-knead and divide the dough into two. Form each piece into an oblong, then roll up like a Swiss Roll. Place in two well-greased 1lb. loaf tins. Cover and prove until doubled in size. Bake at 375°F/190°C/Gas Mark 5 for 40–50 minutes.

When cooked brush tops of loaves with honey. Cool on a wire tray.

RAISIN BROWN BREAD

12oz./300g raisins
1oz./25g fresh yeast *or*
  1 tbsp./20ml dried yeast
  plus 1 tsp./5ml caster
  sugar
½ pint/250ml milk
2fl.oz./50ml black treacle

6oz./150g margarine or
  butter
6oz./150g brown sugar
1lb./400g wholemeal flour
1lb./400g rye flour
1½ tsp./7.5ml salt

Soak the raisins in boiling water for 20 minutes. Drain. Froth the dried yeast with sugar in ¼ pint/125ml warmed milk *or* crumble the fresh yeast into the milk. Put the remaining milk into a pan with the black treacle and fat and heat gently. Do not boil. Stir in the brown sugar. Remove from heat and allow to cool slightly.

Place the raisins into a bowl, add the flour and salt and mix well. Making a well in the centre, add all the liquid, and mix until all ingredients are incorporated. Knead until the dough is smooth and elastic. Cover and leave in a warm place to rise until almost doubled in bulk. Re-knead on a well-floured surface. Shape to fit two 1lb. loaf tins. Cover and prove for approximately 45 minutes.

Bake at 375°F/190°C/Gas Mark 5 for approximately 1 hour and cool in the tins.

BARM BRACK

This is the Irish version of the Welsh Bara Brith. Half white and half wholemeal flour may be used if desired.

½ pint/250ml milk
1oz./25g fresh yeast *or*
  1 tbsp./20ml dried yeast
  plus ½ tsp./2.5ml sugar
2oz./50g butter
1lb./400g strong plain
  flour
½ tsp./2.5ml salt

2oz./50g caster sugar
1 tsp./5ml grated nutmeg
½ tsp./2.5ml cinnamon
4oz./100g sultanas
4oz./100g currants
2oz./50g chopped peel
Milk to glaze

Follow the method for white bread (see page 18), rubbing the butter into the sifted flour, salt, sugar and spices. Add the fruit to the flour before adding the yeast liquid. Knead, cover and leave to rise for the first time. Re-knead the dough, divide in half and place in two greased 1lb. loaf tins. Cover and leave in a warm place to prove. Brush with milk. Bake at 400°F/200°C/Gas Mark 6 for approximately 30 minutes. Cool on a wire rack. Serve sliced with butter.

APRICOT AND WALNUT BREAD

White
½oz./15g fresh yeast *or*
    2 tsp./10ml dried yeast
    plus 1 tsp./5ml caster
    sugar
½ pint/250ml tepid water
1lb./400g strong plain
    flour
1 tsp./5ml salt
2oz./50g margarine
3oz./75g brown sugar
4oz./100g walnuts,
    coarsely chopped
6oz./150g dried apricots,
    coarsely chopped

Wholemeal
½oz./15g fresh yeast *or*
    2 tsp./10ml dried yeast
    plus 1 tsp./5ml sugar
12fl.oz./300ml tepid water
1lb./400g wholemeal flour
1 tsp./5ml salt
3oz./75g margarine
3oz./75g brown sugar
4oz./100g walnuts,
    coarsely chopped
6oz./150g dried apricots,
    coarsely chopped

Glaze
1oz./25g sugar
2 tbsp./40ml water

Follow the method for white bread (see page 18), rubbing the margarine into the flour and mixing in the brown sugar. Cover and leave to rise until doubled in size. Work in the walnuts and apricots, divide the dough in half and shape to fit two 1lb. greased loaf tins and allow to rise again until almost doubled in size. Bake 400°F/200°C/Gas Mark 6 for approximately 35 minutes.

Make the glaze by boiling the sugar and water together for 1 minute, and brush the loaves whilst still hot.

APPLE BREAD

1oz./25g fresh yeast *or*
    1 tbsp./20ml dried yeast
    plus 1 tsp./2.5ml caster
    sugar
8fl.oz./200ml warm milk
4oz./100g margarine,
    rubbed in
1lb./400g plain flour
pinch salt
3oz./75g caster sugar

Topping
2lb./1kg cooking apples
2–4oz./50–100g brown
    sugar

Follow the method for white bread (see page 18), adding the sugar to the fat and flour. Knead, cover and leave in a warm place to rise for the first time.

Divide the dough in half and roll out to fit two 7 inch/18cm square tins. Place dough in bottom of the greased tins. Cover and leave in a warm place to prove. Meanwhile peel, core and slice the apple and layer onto the proved dough. Put into a pre-heated oven at 400°F/200°C/Gas Mark 6. After 10 minutes reduce to 375°F/190°C/Gas Mark 5, sprinkle with the sugar, and bake for approximately 1 hour until the apples are soft and dough cooked.

MUFFINS

To be enjoyed at their best muffins must be eaten fresh.

½oz./15g fresh yeast *or*
    2 tsp./10ml dried yeast
    plus 1 tsp./5ml caster
    sugar.
¼ pint/125ml warm milk
1lb./400g strong plain
    flour

1 tsp./5ml salt
3oz./75g margarine,
    rubbed in
1oz./25g caster sugar
2 eggs, beaten

Follow the method for white bread (see page 18), mixing the sugar into the flour and fat. Make a well in the centre of the flour, add the yeast liquid and beaten eggs and mix to form a dough. Knead until smooth and elastic. Cover and leave in a warm place for 1 hour or until the dough has doubled in bulk. Re-knead the mixture and roll out to ½ inch/12mm thick and cut into rounds using a 2½ inch/6cm plain cutter. Place on a greased baking sheet and bake at 400°F/200°C/Gas Mark 6 for approximately 15 minutes, or until they sound hollow when the bases are tapped. Cool on a wire rack.

To serve pull open muffins all round the edges with fingers, toast slowly on both sides, then pull fully apart and fill with slices of very cold butter. Do not spread the butter. Put the halves together again. Serve warm.

CRUMPETS

Crumpets can vary in size from a large dinner plate to the small, rather holey crumpet made in the Midlands.

½oz./15g fresh yeast *or*
  2 tsp./10ml dried yeast
  plus ½ tsp./2.5ml caster
  sugar
¾ pint/375 ml warm water
12oz./300g strong plain
  flour

1 tsp./5ml salt
¼ pint/125ml warm milk
½ tsp./2.5ml bicarbonate
  of soda

Froth the dried yeast in the warm water with sugar, *or* crumble fresh yeast into the water. Make a smooth batter with the yeast liquid and the sifted flour and salt. Place the batter in a warm place for 1–1½ hours until a good froth has formed.

Add the warm milk and stir well. Sprinkle the bicarbonate of soda onto the batter and stir in well. Cover and allow to stand for 30 minutes until it begins to froth again. Lightly grease a frying pan and 3 inch/7cm diameter pastry cutters. Pre-heat the pan and place in the cutters. Pour 2–3 tbsp./40–60ml batter into each cutter. Gently cook the crumpets over a moderate heat for 5–10 minutes, until the top surface of the crumpet is set and the base is golden brown. Remove the cutters and turn crumpets. Brown the top surface for 2–3 minutes to cook the crumpets through. Cool on a wire rack and then grill. Serve hot with butter.

Crumpets are delicious toasted on the end of a brass fork over an open fire, then buttered liberally.
Makes approximately 15 crumpets.

FRUIT BUNS

Half white and half wholemeal flour may be used for this recipe.

1oz./25g fresh yeast *or*
  1 tbsp./20ml dried yeast
  plus 1 tsp./5ml caster
  sugar
1 egg, beaten and made up
  to ½ pint/250ml with
  milk and water
1lb./400g strong plain
  flour
½ tsp./2.5ml salt

3oz./75g caster sugar
3oz./75g margarine,
  softened
4oz./100g currants
4oz./100g sultanas

Glaze
1 small egg
½ tsp./2.5ml sugar
2 tsp./10ml water

Follow the method for white bread (see page 18), frothing yeast in warm milk and egg, adding sugar with flour, knead and leave to rise. Add the fruit and re-knead. Divide the dough into six pieces and shape into buns on a well-floured board. Place on a greased tray well apart. Cover and leave to prove. Prepare the glaze by mixing the egg, sugar and water together. Brush buns with glaze. Bake at 425°F/220°C/Gas Mark 7 for 15–20 minutes. If smaller fruit buns are desired, shape the dough into smaller pieces: 12 buns will take 10–15 minutes at 425°F/220°C/Gas Mark 7.
Makes approximately 6 large buns.

HOT CROSS BUNS

Traditionally served on Good Friday, Hot Cross Buns are the descendants of Wheaten Cakes eaten at the pre-Christian Spring festival.

1oz./25g fresh yeast *or*
  1 tbsp./20ml dried yeast
3oz./75g caster sugar
1lb./400g strong plain
  flour
½ tsp./2.5ml salt
½ tsp./2.5ml ground
  nutmeg
1 tsp./5ml ground
  cinnamon
1 tsp./5ml mixed spice
3oz./75g margarine
1 egg, beaten made up to
  ½ pint/250ml with milk
  and water
4oz./100g currants
2oz./50g chopped mixed
  peel

Paste
1oz./25g margarine
2oz./50g plain flour
4 tbsp./80ml water

Glaze
1½oz./40g caster sugar
3fl.oz./75ml milk and
  water

Froth the dried yeast in the warm liquid with 1 tsp./5ml of the sugar, *or* crumble the fresh yeast into the warm liquid. Sift the remaining sugar, flour, salt and spices together and rub in the margarine. Make a well in the centre of the flour mixture and pour in the yeast liquid and mix to form a dough. Knead the dough until smooth and elastic. Cover and leave in a warm place to rise for the first time. Add the fruit and re-knead. Divide the dough into 16 pieces and shape into buns. Place well apart on a greased baking tray. Cover and prove. To make the crosses, mix the paste ingredients together well. Brush the buns with a little milk, cut crosses on the tops with the tip of a sharp knife. Pipe the paste over the cross using a fine plain nozzle. Bake at 425°F/220°C/Gas Mark 7 for 15–20 minutes.

While the buns are cooking prepare the glaze by dissolving the ingredients over a gentle heat. Boil for about 2 minutes. When buns are golden brown remove from oven onto a wire rack and brush whilst hot with the glaze. Leave to cool.
Makes approximately 16 buns.

PINE NUT AND ORANGE BUNS

4oz./100g sultanas
1fl.oz./25ml sweet white
  wine
½oz./15g fresh yeast *or*
  2 tsp./10ml dried yeast
4fl.oz./100ml warm milk
2oz./50g butter, melted
2oz./50g caster sugar
12oz./300g ordinary plain
  flour
pinch salt

grated rind of 2 oranges
2oz./50g pine kernels
1 egg, beaten
2 tsp./10ml orange juice

Soak the sultanas in the white wine until most of the liquid has been absorbed. Froth the dried yeast in the warmed milk and butter with ½ tsp./2.5ml of the caster sugar *or* crumble the fresh yeast into the milk. Mix the flour, salt, remaining sugar, orange rind, drained sultanas and pine kernels together. Making a well in the centre; pour in the yeast liquid with the egg and orange juice and mix until a soft dough is formed. Knead the dough. Cover with a damp cloth and leave in a warm place for 1 hour or until doubled in bulk. Re-knead, divide into eight or 12 pieces (depending upon size). Shape into rounds, place on greased baking sheets and leave to prove. Glaze with the beaten egg yolk mixed with 2 tbsp./40ml milk. Bake at 400°F/200°C/Gas Mark 6 for approximately 20 minutes. Cool on a wire rack.
Makes 8–12 buns.

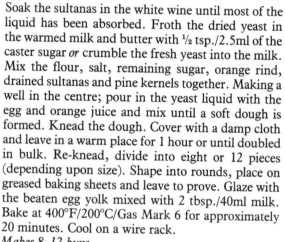

BATH BUNS

Bath Buns were invented by an 18th century Bath physician, Dr Oliver, who treated rich Londoners visiting the Spa. When eaten by his patients, these rich buns undid all the good of his treatment, so Dr Oliver cleverly hit upon the idea of a plain biscuit that was not as fattening as his buns; they are still known as Bath Oliver Biscuits.

1oz./25g fresh yeast *or*
   1 tbsp./20ml dried yeast
   plus 1 tsp./5ml caster
   sugar
¼ pint/125ml milk +
   4 tbsp./80ml water
1lb./400g strong plain
   flour
2oz./50g margarine
1 tsp./5ml salt
2oz./50g mixed peel
6oz./150g sultanas
2oz./50g caster sugar
2 eggs, beaten

Glaze
1 egg beaten with
   1 tsp./5ml caster sugar
1–2oz./25–50g sugar
   lumps, crushed *or*
   preserving sugar

Froth the dried yeast in the liquid with the sugar *or* crumble the fresh yeast into the liquid. Rub the margarine into the sifted flour and salt. Mix in the fruit and sugar. Make a well in the centre of dry ingredients and add the yeast liquid with the eggs, mix to form a soft dough. Knead for 10–15 minutes until smooth and elastic. Cover and leave to rise in a warm place for 1 hour or until doubled in size. When ready, beat well, and place approximately 20 spoonfuls of the mixture onto greased baking sheets. Cover and allow to rise until doubled in size. Prepare the glaze and brush the buns with it, sprinkle with the crushed sugar. Bake in a pre-heated oven at 375°F/190°C/Gas Mark 5 for approximately 15 minutes until golden brown. Cool on a wire rack.
Makes approximately 20 buns.

CHELSEA BUNS

George II, George III and George IV bought buns from the famous Chelsea Bun House in Grosvenor Row during the 18th century.

2oz./50g strong plain flour
½oz./15g fresh yeast *or*
   2 tsp./10ml dried yeast
4fl.oz./100ml warm milk
6oz./150g strong flour *or*
   2oz./50g strong plain
   and 4oz./100g
   wholemeal flour
½ tsp./2.5ml salt
½ tsp./2.5ml caster sugar
½oz./15g butter, *or*
   margarine *or* lard
1 egg, beaten

Filling
2oz./50g butter, melted
3oz./75g dried fruit
1oz./25g mixed peel
2oz./50g soft brown sugar

Glaze
honey

Blend 2oz./50g flour, the yeast and milk together in a large bowl and put aside for about 20–30 minutes or until the mixture froths. Sieve the 6oz./150g flour, salt and sugar and rub in the fat. Make a well in the centre and pour in yeast batter, beaten eggs and beat until a soft dough forms.

Knead until smooth and elastic. Cover and leave in a warm place to rise for ¾–1 hour or until the mixture has doubled in bulk. Lightly knead the dough and roll to a rectangle 12 × 9 inches/30 × 22.5cm. Brush the surface with melted butter and then sprinkle on the dried fruit, mixed peel and brown sugar.

Roll up from the longest side, like a Swiss Roll, and seal the edges. Cut into nine equal slices and place these, cut side downwards, on a lightly greased baking tray well apart, or in a 7 inch/18cm square tin.

Cover and leave to rise in a warm place for about 30 minutes until the dough feels springy and has doubled in size.

Bake at 375°F/190°C/Gas Mark 5 for 20–25 minutes on a baking tray or 30–35 minutes in a tin. Cool on a wire rack. Brush with honey.
Makes 9 buns.

YORKSHIRE TEA CAKES

½oz./15g fresh yeast *or*
  2 tsp./10ml dried yeast
  plus ½ tsp./2.5ml caster
  sugar
½ pint/250ml milk,
  warmed

1lb./400g strong plain
  flour or 8oz./200g white
  and 8oz./200g
  wholemeal flour
1oz./25g caster sugar
1 tsp./5ml salt
2oz./50g currants
1oz./25g mixed peel
1oz./25g lard

Follow the method for white bread (see page 18), adding the fruit with the dry ingredients. Knead until smooth and cover with a damp cloth and leave in a warm place for 1 hour or until doubled in bulk. Re-knead and shape into five circles about 5 inches/13cm in diameter. Place on a greased baking sheet and prove. Bake at 400°F/200°C/Gas Mark 6 for 20 minutes. Cool on a wire rack.
Makes 5 tea cakes.

JAM DOUGHNUTS

1oz./25g fresh yeast *or*
  1 tbsp./20ml dried yeast
  plus 1 tsp./5ml sugar
8fl.oz./200ml warm water
12oz./300g ordinary plain
  flour

2oz./50g butter or
  margarine
½ tsp./2.5ml salt
2oz./50g caster sugar
jam to fill
caster sugar to finish

Froth the dried yeast with 1 tsp./5ml of the sugar in the water for approximately 15 minutes, *or* crumble the fresh yeast into the water. Rub fat into the flour, salt and sugar and add the yeast liquid. Beat rather than knead to a smooth, fairly soft dough. Cover and leave in a warm place to rise until doubled in bulk. With floured hands shape the dough into balls 1½ inches/3cm in diameter. Place on a floured baking tray, cover and prove.

Pre-heat a deep pan of oil to 190°C, when a cube of day old bread browns in 1 minute. Deep-fry the doughnuts until golden brown, about 10 minutes. Drain on kitchen paper, make a small slit in the side of each and insert 1 tsp./5ml jam. Roll in caster sugar.
Makes approximately 18 doughnuts.

BANBURY CAKES

These cakes from Oxfordshire date back to late 16th century. They are best eaten fresh from the oven and still warm. Although they are sometimes made with shortcrust, this recipe uses yeast pastry.

Pastry
½oz./15g fresh yeast *or*
  2 tsp./10ml dried yeast
  plus ½ tsp./2.5ml sugar
½ pint/250ml warm water
1lb./400g ordinary plain
  flour
2 tsp./10ml salt
½oz./15g lard
6oz./150g lard and
  margarine, cut into
  small pieces

Filling
2oz./50g butter
½oz./15g plain flour
2oz./50g soft brown sugar
½ tsp./2.5ml mixed spice
1oz./25g chopped peel
4oz./100g currants

Glaze
milk

Froth the dried yeast with the caster sugar in the warmed water, *or* crumble the fresh yeast in the warmed water. Rub the lard into the flour and salt; add the yeast liquid and knead until smooth and elastic. Cover the dough and put in a warm place for 1 hour to rise until doubled in bulk.

Roll out dough to an oblong ¾ inch/2cm thick. Dot one third of fat in little pats onto the dough, and flour lightly. Fold dough in three and press edges together. Turn through 90 degrees, cover and leave to rest for 15 minutes in fridge. Repeat with the remaining margarine and lard. Cover and leave the pastry until required in the fridge or cold place.

Prepare the filling by gently melting the butter. Remove from the heat and stir in the flour. Return to heat and cook for a couple of minutes. Add the remaining ingredients. Leave to cool.

Roll out pastry to approximately ¼ inch/6mm thick, cut into 3 inch/7.5cm rounds. Put a little of the mixture on each, damp the edges, and draw together. Pinch firmly and turn over. Shape cakes into ovals, making slits on the top with a knife. Place onto a greased baking tray, brush with milk and sprinkle with caster sugar.

Bake at 425°F/220°C/Gas Mark 7 for approximately 20 minutes or until cooked.
Makes approximately 25 cakes.

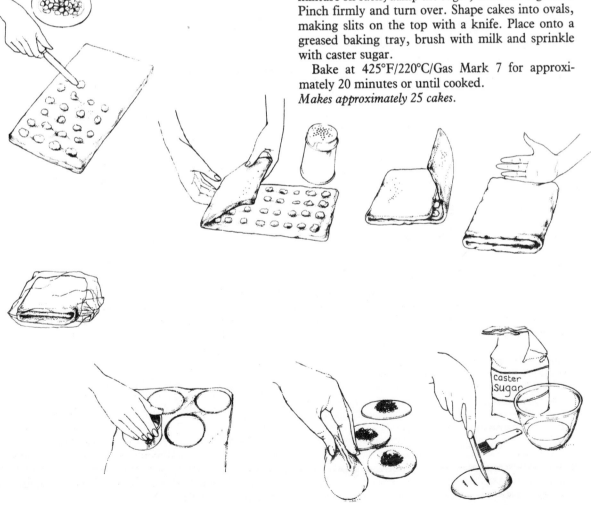

LARDY CAKE

½oz./15g fresh yeast *or*
  2 tsp./10ml dried yeast
  plus ½ tsp./2.5ml caster
  sugar
½ pint/250ml warm milk
1 tbsp./20ml oil
1lb./400g strong plain
  flour
1 tsp./5ml salt

2oz./50g butter, cut into
  pieces
2oz./50g lard, cut into
  pieces
4oz./100g caster sugar
4oz./100g currants and
  sultanas
½ tsp./2.5mg mixed spice

Follow the method for white bread (see page 18), adding the oil with the yeast liquid to give a manageable dough. After the first rising, roll out the dough into an oblong ¼ inch/6mm thick. Cover two-thirds of the dough with small flakes of butter and lard and 3 tbsp./60ml sugar. Mix the spice and fruit together and sprinkle half the mixture onto the dough. Fold in three, seal the edges with a rolling pin and give the dough a half turn. Roll into an oblong and repeat the procedure with the remaining fat, spice and fruit mixture. Fold in three, turn and roll into an oblong once more. Place in a greased tin 10 × 8 inches/25 × 20cm so that the dough fills the corners. Cover and prove until doubled in bulk. Brush top with oil and sprinkle on remaining sugar and make a criss-cross pattern across the top. Bake at 425°F/220°C/Gas Mark 7 for 30 minutes. Cool on a wire rack.

Alternative Topping
Boil 1oz./25g granulated sugar with 2 tbsp./40ml milk until syrupy. Brush the glaze on the hot Lardy Cake.

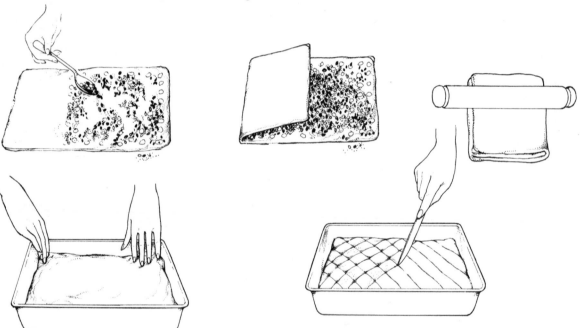

SAFFRON CAKE

This cake is traditionally made in the West Country.

good pinch of powdered
  saffron
¼ pint/125ml warm water
½oz./15g fresh yeast *or*
  1½ tsp./7.5ml dried
  yeast plus 1 tsp./5ml
  caster sugar
½ pint/250ml warm milk
  and water
5oz./125g lard
1lb.8oz./600g strong plain
  flour *or* 12oz./300g
  strong plain and

12oz./300g wholemeal
  flour
1 tsp./5ml salt
2oz./50g caster sugar
4oz./100g currants
2oz./50g sultanas
2oz./50g chopped mixed
  peel
½ tsp./2.5ml grated
  nutmeg

Dissolve the saffron in the ¼ pint/125ml warm water. Dissolve the fresh yeast in the milk and water *or* froth the dried yeast and sugar in the warm milk and water.

Rub the fat into the flour and salt, then add the sugar, dried fruit, peel and nutmeg. Add the saffron liquid and yeast liquid to the dry ingredients and mix to form a soft dough. Cover dough with a damp cloth and leave to rise in a warm place for 1–1½ hours or until doubled in bulk. Re-knead the dough, divide it into two pieces and shape to fit two well-greased 6 inch/15cm round cake tins. Prove the dough and bake at 400°F/200°C/Gas Mark 6 for 35–40 minutes. Cool on a wire rack.

SIMNEL YEAST CAKE

Originally the Simnel yeast cake, with a layer of almond paste baked through the middle, was made for Mothering Sunday. As time went on the almond paste was moved from the middle to the top to make an Easter Cake. In this recipe the almond paste runs through the middle in the traditional way.

½oz./15g fresh yeast *or*
  2 tsp./10ml dried yeast
  plus ½ tsp./5ml caster
  sugar
3fl.oz./75ml warm milk
3oz./75g margarine or
  butter
12oz./300g strong plain
  flour
1 tsp./5ml salt
1 tsp./5ml mixed spice
1½oz./40g brown sugar
2 eggs, beaten
6oz./150g currants
1½oz./40g chopped mixed
  peel

Almond Paste
6oz./150g ground almonds
3oz./75g icing sugar
3oz./75g caster sugar
1 egg, beaten
almond essence

Froth the dried yeast with ½ tsp./5ml sugar in the warm milk, *or* crumble the fresh yeast into the warm milk. Rub the fat into the flour, add the salt, yeast liquid, spice, sugar, fruit and eggs. Knead the dough until smooth and elastic. Cover and leave in a warm place for 1 hour or until doubled in bulk.

To make the almond paste combine the ground almonds, icing sugar and caster sugar together with sufficient egg and a few drops of almond essence to make a stiff dough. Form into a ball and roll out into a circle 8 inches/20cm in diameter.

Divide the yeast mixture in half, roll out each half to fit a greased 8 inches/20cm round loose bottomed cake tin. Place half the dough in the tin, then place the layer of marzipan on the top, cover with final layer of yeast mixture. Cover and leave to rise until doubled in bulk.

Bake at 425°F/220°C/Gas Mark 7 for 10 minutes, then turn oven down to 350°F/180°C/Gas Mark 4 for a further 30–40 minutes. The Simnel Cake should be nicely browned, and the base firm. Cool on a wire rack.

BRAN-TOPPED ORANGE CAKE

12oz./300g wholemeal
  flour
½ tsp./2.5ml salt
3oz./75g caster sugar
1oz./25g fresh yeast *or*
  ½oz./15g dried yeast
5oz./125g margarine

4oz./100g sultanas
2 oranges
2 eggs
4 tbsp./75ml warm milk
2 tbsp./40ml orange
  marmalade
1oz./25g brown sugar
½ tsp./2.5ml cinnamon

Sieve the flour and reserve the bran. Place the flour, salt and sugar into a bowl, crumble in the fresh yeast and rub in the margarine. If using dried yeast, froth it in the warm milk with 1tsp./5ml sugar. Add the sultanas, grated rind and juice of the oranges, eggs, and milk and mix together well. Turn into a greased and lined 2lb. loaf tin and smooth over the surface.

Carefully spread the marmalade over the surface of the cake. If the marmalade is a very stiff jelly, warm it slightly first. Mix the sugar, cinnamon and reserved bran together and sprinkle evenly over the marmalade. Leave the cake to prove until it reaches the top of the tin (approximately 1 hour in a warm place). Bake in a pre-heated oven at 400°F/200°C/Gas Mark 6 for 35–40 minutes. Use a skewer to test when cooked. Remove cake from tin and cool on a wire rack.

DOUGH CAKES

½oz./15g fresh yeast *or*
 2 tsp./10ml dried yeast
 plus ½ tsp./2.5ml caster
 sugar
½ pint/250ml milk and
 water
1oz./25g butter
1lb./400g strong plain
 flour
½ tsp./2.5ml salt

5oz./125g mixed dried
 fruit
2oz./50g caster sugar
1 tsp./5ml mixed spice
grated rind of 1 orange

Glaze
honey

Follow the recipe for white bread (see page 18) first rubbing the butter into the sifted flour and salt. Knead, cover and leave to rise in a warm place for 1 hour or until doubled in size.

Re-knead the dough, incorporating the dried fruit, caster sugar, spice and grated orange rind.

Shape the mixture to fit two 1lb. loaf tins. Prove, and bake at 400°F/200°C/Gas Mark 6 for 25–30 minutes.

Remove from the oven and brush loaves with honey. Cool on a wire rack.

SOURDOUGH

The pioneers making their way across the new lands of North America carried with them a pot of sourdough starter. The method of leavening known as 'sourdough' was used because the fresh yeast available at that time spoiled easily. A batch of bread would be made conventionally. Before baking, a ball of this dough was set to one side in a covered bowl for about four days to become 'sour'. This was known as the 'starter' and formed the basis of the new batch of bread. From each batch of bread a fresh starter was reserved, and in this way the method was perpetuated. This starter was required for all risen foods on the trail, and became a valued family possession, guarded jealously through both good and bad times.

Method
Make up a batch of white bread (see page 18) and reserve a fair piece of the dough, weighing 1–1¼lb./400–500g for your 'starter'. Cover the bowl of dough with a cloth and leave in a warm place for 3–4 days. By this time the dough should have a pleasant sour smell.

Mix this soured dough with 1lb./400g flour, either rye or wheat, and ¾ pint/375ml warm water. Leave the batter in a covered bowl overnight. The dough is now ready to use. (If you wish to make sourdough bread in the future, reserve enough dough to fill a jam jar; kept covered in a cool place, it will last for about one week.) To the dough add the following ingredients:

3 tbsp./60ml honey
2 tsp./10ml salt
½ pint/250ml milk
2lb./800g flour e.g. a
 mixture of wheat and rye.

Knead the dough until it is smooth and elastic; it may be easier to do this in two batches. Shape into two loaves and place on greased baking sheets. Oil the loaves, cover, and leave to double in bulk. Bake at 400°F/200°C/Gas Mark 6 for 30 minutes; reduce heat to 375°F/190°C/Gas Mark 5 for a further 10 minutes until cooked.

CORN BREAD (AMERICAN MUFFINS)

These muffins are traditionally served hot for breakfast in America. They are not bread in the true sense as baking powder is used to raise the dough.

8oz./200g maize meal
6oz./150g wholemeal flour
2 tsp./10ml caster sugar
½ tsp./2.5ml salt
1 tsp./5ml baking powder

3oz./75g butter or
 margarine
2 eggs, separated
2½fl.oz./65ml single cream
½ pint/250ml milk

Mix the maize meal, wholemeal flour, sugar, salt, and baking powder together. Rub in the fat. Blend the egg yolks, cream and milk together and add to the dry ingredients. Whisk the egg whites until stiff and carefully fold into the mixture. Put into greased muffin or bun tins, filling each three-quarters full. Bake at 400°F/200°C/Gas Mark 6 for approximately 25 minutes. Turn out and cool on a wire rack.
Makes approximately 18 muffins.

ANADAMA BREAD

The story goes that this bread was invented by a New England farmer who, tired of his daily diet of corn-meal and molasses, took the bowl from his wife, added yeast and flour and proceeded to make this into bread on the hearth. On tasting it, he cried, 'There, Anna, dammit this is what I like!'

1¼lb./500g strong plain
  flour
2oz./50g maize meal
1 tsp./5ml salt
1oz./25g fresh yeast *or*
  1 tbsp./20ml dried yeast
  plus 1 tsp./5ml caster
  sugar

4oz./100g butter or
  margarine
3oz./75g golden syrup
½ pint/250ml water
4fl.oz./100ml warm water

Heat ½ pint/250ml water, maize meal, salt, butter and golden syrup until the mixture thickens. Pour into a bowl and leave to cool until lukewarm.

Froth the dried yeast and sugar in 4fl.oz./100ml of warm water *or* crumble the fresh yeast into warm water and leave for 10 minutes. Add to the cooled maize mixture. Beat in the flour and then knead until smooth and elastic.

Cover the dough with a damp cloth and leave in a warm place for 1 hour or until doubled in bulk. Re-knead and shape to fit a greased 2lb. loaf tin. Cover and prove again. Bake at 375°F/190°C/Gas Mark 5 for approximately 50 minutes. Remove from tin and cool on a wire rack.

PEANUT BUTTER BREAD

½oz./15g fresh yeast *or*
  2 tsp./10ml dried yeast
  plus 1 tsp./5ml caster
  sugar
8fl.oz./200ml warm water
2 tbsp./40ml honey

1lb./400g wholemeal flour
1 tsp./5ml salt
2 tbsp./40ml low-fat dried
  milk powder
1 egg, beaten
4oz./100g peanut butter

Froth the dried yeast *or* crumble the fresh yeast in the warm water with the honey. Mix the flour, salt and dried milk powder together. Add the yeast liquid, beaten egg and peanut butter and mix until the dough comes cleanly from the sides of the bowl. Knead the dough until smooth and elastic. Cover with a damp cloth and leave in a warm place for 1 hour or until doubled in bulk. Shape and put into two greased 1lb. loaf tins. Cover and prove. Bake at 375°F/190°C/Gas Mark 5 for 30 minutes. Cool on a wire rack.

PITKA

Pitka is a Bulgarian bread containing tiny pieces of white goat's cheese. In Bulgaria it is sold freshly-baked from round tins at practically every street corner and is always served in restaurants. As goat's cheese is difficult to buy in this country, cottage cheese is used for this recipe.

½oz./15g fresh yeast *or*
  2 tsp./10ml dried yeast
  plus ½ tsp./2.5ml caster
  sugar
3 tbsp./60ml warm water
½ pint/250ml warm milk
3 tsp./15ml salt

1½lb./600g ordinary plain
  flour
1 large egg, beaten
2 tbsp./40ml salad oil
4oz./100g cottage cheese at
  room temperature
Beaten egg for glazing

Follow the method for white bread (see page 18), adding the egg and oil to the yeast liquid. Cover and leave dough to double in bulk. Re-knead, mixing in the cheese at the same time. Divide into three and shape each piece to fill a 7 inch/18cm greased sandwich tin. Prove until dough is almost doubled in bulk. Brush with beaten egg. Bake at 425°F/220°C/Gas Mark 7 for 25–30 minutes until the base of the loaf sounds hollow when tapped. Cool on a wire rack. This bread should be eaten warm.

DANISH PASTRIES

½oz./15g fresh yeast *or*
  2 tsp./10ml dried yeast
  plus ½ tsp./2.5ml caster
  sugar
6 tbsp./120ml warm water

8oz./200g ordinary plain
  flour
pinch salt
½oz./15g caster sugar
1 egg, beaten
6oz./150g butter

Froth the dried yeast with ½ tsp./2.5mg caster sugar in 6 tbsp./120ml warm water *or* crumble the fresh yeast in the same amount of liquid. Sift flour and salt together, add sugar. Mix the beaten egg with the yeast mixture and pour into the flour. Mix to a soft dough and work lightly together. Leave to rest for 10–15 minutes in a cool place. Cut the butter into eight slices approximately ¼ inch/6mm thick (this should be only just soft enough to cut) and leave in a cool place.

Roll out the dough to approximately 8 × 15 inches/20 × 38cm. Place the dough on a working surface with the longest side towards you and arrange four butter slices in the middle (see diagram 1). Fold left-hand half over the butter sealing edges (see diagram 2), arrange remaining butter slices on top of folded dough, and then fold the right-hand side on top (see diagram 3).

Roll the folded dough to a rectangle 16 × 6 inches/40 × 15cm. Place longest side towards you and fold both the ends into the centre (see diagram 4). Bring the right half of the dough on top of the left to make four layers of dough (see diagram 5). Leave to rest in a cool place for 30 minutes.

Roll dough out to 16 × 6 inches/40 × 15cm and repeat folding. Leave for further 30 minutes. Repeat folding again and leave for at least 2 hours or overnight in a cool place.

The dough may be rolled out in the following traditional shapes:

Windmills

1oz./25g ground almonds
1oz./25g caster sugar
few drops of almond
  essence
little beaten egg

Prepare the almond paste by mixing all the ingredients together well. Roll out half the quantity of dough into an oblong 6 × 12 inches/15 × 30cm. Cut the dough into 3 inch/7.5cm squares. Place a small knob of almond paste on each square. Make short diagonal cuts across the square and fold up as shown in diagram.
Makes 8.

Tivolis

½ small cooking apple,
  peeled and finely
  chopped
1 tbsp./20ml demerara or
  soft brown sugar
1 tbsp./20ml mixed peel

Prepare the filling by mixing all the ingredients together. Roll out half the dough into an oblong 6 × 12 inches/15 × 30cm. Cut the dough into 3 inch/7.5cm squares. Place a heaped teaspoon of filling on each square and fold up as shown in diagram.
Makes 8.

Envelopes

1 quantity almond paste
  (see previous page)

Prepare the almond paste. Using half the dough roll out to an oblong 12 × 8 inches/30 × 20cm. Cut the dough into 3 inch/7.2cm squares. Place a small knob of almond paste in the centre of each square and fold up as shown in diagram.
Makes 8.

Cockscombs

3 tbsp./60ml milk
¼oz./7.5g cornflour
½oz./15g caster sugar
½ egg yolk
a few drops of vanilla
  essence.

Prepare the vanilla cream by blending all the ingredients together. Heat in a pan, stirring all the time, until the mixture has thickened. Using half the quantity of dough roll out an oblong 8 × 12 inches/20 × 30cm. Cut dough into oblongs 4 × 3 inches/9 × 7.5cm. Spread a teaspoon of the vanilla cream in the centre of each oblong. Fold and cut as shown in diagram.
Makes 8.

Snails

1oz./25g butter
1oz./25g caster sugar
1 tsp./5ml ground
  cinnamon

Prepare the cinnamon paste by mixing all the ingredients together well. Using half the dough roll out and cut into strips 2 × 12 inches/5 × 30cm. Spread the cinnamon paste over the strips. Roll up from the shorter end and cut each piece twice almost through to the base. Open the cut pieces out like a fan.
Makes 16.

Cartwheels

1 quantity of almond paste
  (see above)
3–4 glacé cherries,
  chopped

Prepare the almond paste. Using half the dough roll out to strips 12 × 2 inches/30 × 5cm. Spread the almond paste over the strips and sprinkle on the chopped cherries. Roll up and split into two pieces and place cut side up on a baking sheet. See diagram.
Makes 16.

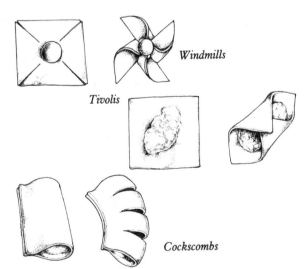

Windmills

Tivolis

Cockscombs

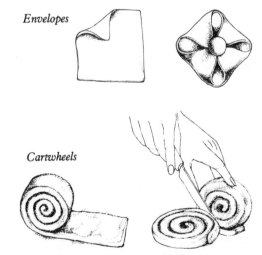

Envelopes

Cartwheels

After shaping pastries, leave to prove for 20 minutes or until puffy. Bake at 425°F/220°C/Gas Mark 7 for 10–15 minutes.

The cooked pastries may be topped with *either* an apricot glaze: 4 tbsp./80ml apricot jam plus 8 tbsp./160ml water boiled together for 3 minutes until thickened *or* glacé icing: 2oz./50g icing sugar blended to a coating consistency with a few drops of lemon juice. Use chopped nuts or glacé cherries as an additional topping.

MORAVARIAN LOAF

This is a Czechoslovakian recipe containing mashed potato.

½oz./15g fresh yeast *or*
  2 tsp./10ml dried yeast
  plus ½ tsp./2.5ml caster
  sugar
¼ pint/125ml warm water
1½lb./600g ordinary plain
  flour
1 tsp./5ml salt
1 tsp./5ml ground
  cinnamon

5oz./125g caster sugar
5oz./125g margarine or
  butter
8oz./200g cooked and
  mashed potato
2oz./50g caster sugar
2 tsp./10ml ground
  nutmeg
pinch ground mace

Froth the dried yeast and sugar in the warm water *or* crumble the fresh yeast into the warm water. Sift flour, salt, cinnamon and sugar into a bowl and rub in 3oz./75g of the fat. Add the mashed potato and mix well. Add the yeast mixture and knead until the dough is smooth and elastic. Cover the dough with a damp cloth and leave in a warm place for about 2 hours or until doubled in bulk. Re-knead and shape to fit a greased 2lb. loaf tin.

Melt the remaining 2oz./50g fat and brush a small amount lightly over the top of the dough. Cover and leave dough to prove until it has risen almost to the top of the tin. Brush dough again with melted butter during the rising time.

After it has proved make three deep cuts into the top of the dough. Mix the nutmeg and mace and sprinkle into the cuts, using any left over to sprinkle on top of the dough. Pour the remaining butter over the dough.

Bake at 375°F/190°C/Gas Mark 5 for approximately 1 hour or until loaf sounds hollow when tapped. Cool on a wire rack. Serve warm with butter.

KUGELHOPF

Kugelhopf, baked in a special fluted mould, comes from the French province of Alsace across the Rhine from Germany, hence the Germanic name. Although delicious when fresh it quickly stales, but it is then ideal for soaking in warm syrup.

4oz./100g raisins
2 tbsp./40ml Kirsch or
  water
1oz./25g fresh yeast *or*
  1 tbsp./20ml dried yeast
½ pint/250ml warm water
1–2oz./25–50g flaked
  almonds

4oz./100g margarine or
  butter
3oz./75g caster sugar
2 large eggs
14oz./350g ordinary plain
  flour
grated rind of 1 orange
½ tsp./2.5ml salt

Soak the raisins in the Kirsch or water until the liquid has been absorbed.

Froth the dried yeast with ½ tsp./2.5ml of the caster sugar, and warm water *or* crumble the fresh yeast into the liquid.

Thickly butter a 9 inch/22.5cm Kugelhopf tin, and sprinkle with almonds to cover evenly.

Cream the fat with remaining caster sugar and gradually beat in the eggs. Add the flour, yeast liquid, orange rind, salt and raisins, until all the ingredients are incorporated. Put into the prepared tin. Cover with a damp cloth and leave in a warm place to rise until mixture fills the tin. Bake at 400°F/200°C/Gas Mark 6 for 20 minutes and reduce heat to 375°F/190°C/Gas Mark 5 for a further 30–40 minutes. If the top becomes too dark cover with greaseproof paper. Cool on a wire rack.

FRENCH BREAD

It's virtually impossible to re-create the traditional French baguettes in England. They are made with a very soft French flour, risen many times and baked in special ovens. The recipe below is a reasonable copy, but you'll have to travel across the Channel for the real thing.

½oz./15g fresh yeast *or* 2 tsp./10ml dried yeast plus 1 tsp./5ml caster sugar
½ pint/250ml warm water

8oz./200g ordinary plain flour
4oz./100g self raising flour
4oz./100g cornflour
1 tsp./5ml salt
1 egg, beaten to glaze

Crumble the fresh yeast into the water *or* froth the dried yeast with the sugar in the water. Sift the flours, and salt into a bowl, make a well in the centre and add the yeast liquid. Mix to form a soft dough and knead. Cover with a damp cloth and put to rise in a warm place until almost doubled in bulk. Re-knead, and divide in half.

Roll out on a lightly floured surface to a rectangle 12 × 4 inches/30 × 10cm fold in three to make a 4 inch/10cm square. Turn the dough through 90 degrees and roll out and shape twice more. Finally, roll out to oblong 4 × 16 inches/10 × 40cm and roll up into a sausage shape. Place on a floured baking sheet, make diagonal cuts across the dough. Leave to rise again uncovered until doubled in bulk. Brush off flour and glaze with egg slightly diluted with water. Bake at 425°F/220°C/Gas Mark 7 for 20–25 minutes with a roasting tin containing approximately 1 inch/2.5cm of water in the bottom of the oven. Cool on a wire rack. Eat the same day.

GARLIC BREAD

4oz./100g softened butter
1 clove garlic, crushed
1 tbsp./20ml parsley
1 loaf french bread

Cream the butter, with the garlic and parsley. Cut the loaf into thick slices crosswise to within about ¼ inch/6mm of the bottom and spread the butter mixture generously on one side of each slice. Wrap in foil and place on a baking sheet and bake for 15–20 minutes at 400°F/200°C/Gas Mark 6. Serve hot.

ROQUEFORT QUICHE

This recipe uses a yeasted pastry.

Pastry
¼oz./7.5g fresh yeast *or* 1 tsp./5ml dried yeast
5oz./125g strong plain flour
1 tsp./5ml salt
1 egg
3 tbsp./60ml warm milk

Filling
4oz./100g Roquefort cheese
4 tbsp./80ml milk
3 tbsp./60ml double cream
pinch nutmeg
pinch pepper
2 eggs

Froth the dried or fresh yeast in the liquid for 15–20 minutes, add the flour, salt and egg. Knead until dough is smooth and elastic. Cover with a damp cloth and leave for 1 hour or until doubled in bulk. Re-knead, roll out to fit the 10 inch/25cm removable base of a flan tin; place in the tin and work dough to the sides and upwards to form the flan case. Leave for 25 minutes, then work again to shape the flan case.

Mash the cheese, add the cream and stir together. Beat the eggs and milk together and add to the cream and cheese mixture. Put into the flan case. Bake at 425°F/220°C/Gas Mark 7 for 15 minutes, cover with a piece of greaseproof paper, reduce temperature to 375°F/190°C/Gas Mark 5 for 10 minutes. Serve immediately.
Serves 6.

BRIOCHE

Brioche is a cross between bread and cake made with butter and eggs. It is best eaten when freshly baked.

½oz./15g fresh yeast *or*
  2 tsp./10ml dried yeast
  plus ½ tsp./2.5ml caster
  sugar
3 tbsp./60ml warm milk
8oz./200g ordinary plain
  flour

½oz./15g caster sugar
pinch of salt
2oz./50g butter or
  margarine
2 eggs, beaten

Froth the dried yeast in the warm milk with ½ tsp./2.5ml sugar *or* crumble the fresh yeast into warm milk. Sift the flour, sugar and salt into a bowl. Rub in the fat. Add the yeast liquid together with the eggs. Mix together and knead until smooth. Cover with a damp cloth and leave in a warm place for 1 hour or until doubled in bulk.

Re-knead and shape three-quarters of the dough into a ball and place in the bottom of a greased 2 pint/1 litre fluted brioche mould. Press a hole in the centre as far as the tin base and put the remainder of the dough in the middle. Cover and leave the dough to rise again until it is light and wobbles when the tin is shaken. Brush lightly with beaten egg and bake in the middle of the oven at 425°F/220°C/Gas Mark 7 for approximately 15 minutes until golden in colour.

Cool on a wire rack.

SAVARIN

White Recipe
1oz./25g fresh yeast *or*
  1 tbsp./20ml dried yeast
6 tbsp./120ml warm milk
1oz./25g caster sugar
8oz./200g strong plain
  flour
1 tsp./5ml salt
4 eggs, beaten
4oz./100g butter, melted

Half Wholemeal Recipe
1oz./25g fresh yeast *or*
  1 tbsp./20ml dried yeast
6 tbsp./120ml warm milk
1oz./25g caster sugar
4oz./100g strong plain
  flour
4oz./100g wholemeal flour
4 eggs
4oz./100g butter

Syrup
8 tbsp./160ml sugar
½ pint/200ml water
4–6 tbsp./80–120ml rum

To Serve
fresh or canned fruit
whipped cream

Mix the yeast with the warm milk, 1 tsp./5ml of the sugar and 2oz./50g of the flour. (If using the half wholemeal recipe use white flour.) Set aside for 15–20 minutes until frothy.

Sift the remaining flour and salt together and stir in the remaining sugar. Make a well in the centre and pour in the yeast mixture and beaten eggs. Add the melted butter and gradually draw all the ingredients together. Beat thoroughly for about 5 minutes by hand or 1 minute if using a mixer. Half fill a well-buttered 8 inch/20cm deep sided ring mould with the mixture. Leave to rise in a warm place for approximately 30–40 minutes in a lightly oiled polythene bag. Bake towards the top of an oven, pre-heated to 400°F/200°C/Gas Mark 6, for approximately 20 minutes.

Meanwhile, prepare the syrup by dissolving the sugar in the water in a heavy saucepan. Bring to the boil and boil for one minute. Remove from the heat and stir in the rum.

Turn out Savarin onto a dish and prick with a skewer. Pour over hot syrup. Allow to cool, fill centre with fruit and serve with whipped cream.
Serves 8.

CROISSANTS

1oz./25g fresh yeast *or*
  1 tbsp./20ml dried yeast
  plus 2 tsp./10ml caster
  sugar
8fl.oz./200ml warm water
1lb./400g strong plain
  flour
2 tsp./10ml salt
1oz./25g butter
1 egg, beaten
3–4oz./75–100g butter
  (chilled) mixed together
  with 3–4oz./75–100g
  lard (chilled)

Glaze
1 egg
½ tsp./2.5ml sugar
2 tsp./10ml water

Froth the dried yeast and sugar in the water *or* crumble the fresh yeast into the water. Sift the flour and salt into a bowl and rub in 1oz./25g butter. Add the yeast liquid together with the egg and knead as for white bread (see page 18). Roll the dough into a rectangle 20 × 8 inches/50 ×20cm and about ¼ inch/6mm thick.

Divide the mixed fat into three. Use one portion to dot over two-thirds of the dough as for flaky pastry (see page 71). Fold into three, folding the plain third over first. Turn through 90 degrees keeping the fold on the right hand side. Roll out as before and repeat with the other two portions of fat. Cover and leave to rest in a cold place for about 30 minutes. Roll out to a rectangular strip and carry out the rolling and folding three times more. Cover and put to rest in a cold place for a further 30 minutes.

To shape the croissants roll the dough into a rectangle about 22 × 13 inches/55 × 33cm. Cover with a sheet of oiled polythene and leave for 10 minutes. Trim the edges of the dough with a sharp knife to leave a rectangle 21 × 12 inches/52 × 30cm and divide into two lengthwise. Cut each strip into six triangles, each side being 6 inches/15cm.

Prepare the glaze by beating the egg with the sugar and a few drops of water. Brush each triangle with this egg wash and roll loosely towards the point finishing with the tip underneath. Curve into a crescent shape. Place croissants onto a greased baking sheet and brush tops with egg wash. Cover and prove for about 30 minutes. Brush tops again with egg wash. Bake at 425°F/220°C/Gas Mark 7 for 15–20 minutes. *Makes 12 croissants.*

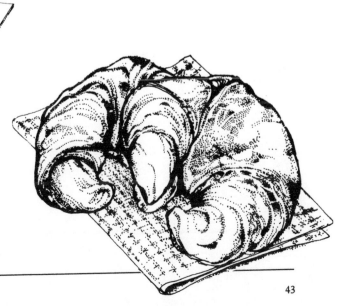

KUCHEN

Kuchen is a traditional cake-bread made in Germany.

½oz./15g fresh yeast *or*
  2 tsp./10ml dried yeast
¼ pint/125ml warm milk
8oz./200g ordinary plain
  flour
½ tsp./2.5ml salt
pinch ground ginger
1oz./25g caster sugar
grated rind of 1 lemon
1 egg, beaten
2oz./50g melted butter

Topping
1 tbsp./20ml apricot jam
2oz./50g digestive biscuits,
  crushed
1oz./25g caster sugar
1 tsp./5ml ground
  cinnamon
1oz./25g melted butter

Froth the dried yeast with ½ tsp./2.5ml sugar dissolved in the warm milk, *or* crumble the fresh yeast into the warm milk. Sift the flour, salt and ground ginger together, add the remaining sugar and lemon rind. Add the yeast liquid with the egg and melted butter.

Beat the dough (this will be too slack to knead). Cover and leave in a warm place to rise until doubled in bulk.

Beat the dough again, and shape to fit a greased 2lb. loaf tin ensuring that the dough fits into the corners of the tin and has a flat top. Spread the top of the dough with the jam. Mix all the other topping ingredients together and spread over the jam. Cover and prove.

Bake at 350°F/180°C/Gas Mark 4 for 40 minutes. Cool on a wire rack.

STOLLEN

Stollen is a traditional folded fruit bread from Germany.

½oz./15g fresh yeast *or*
  2 tsp./10ml dried yeast
  plus ½ tsp./2.5ml caster
  sugar
3fl.oz./75ml warm milk
8oz./200g ordinary plain
  flour
½ tsp./2.5ml salt
1oz./25g margarine
1oz./25g caster sugar

1oz./25g chopped almonds
1oz./25g chopped glacé
  cherries
1oz./25g currants
1oz./25g chopped mixed
  peel
1oz./25g sultanas
1 egg, beaten
grated rind of 1 lemon
icing sugar to dust

Froth the dried yeast with ½ tsp./2.5ml sugar in the warm milk *or* crumble the fresh yeast in the warm liquid. Sift the flour and salt together and rub in the margarine and stir in the caster sugar. Add the prepared fruit and nuts. Make a well in the centre of the flour mixture and pour in the yeast liquid, lemon rind and the beaten egg. Mix to give a soft dough. Knead the dough, cover and leave in a warm place for 1 hour or until doubled in bulk. Re-knead and shape by rolling to an oblong 10 × 8 inches/25 × 20cm. Fold over lengthwise so top is 1 inch/2.5cm from edge of bottom and press down lightly. Place on a greased baking sheet, cover and prove. Bake at 375°F/190°C/Gas Mark 5 for 25–30 minutes. Cool on a wire rack. When cooled dust with icing sugar.

CONTINENTAL SWEET BREAD DOUGH

6oz./150g margarine
1¾ pints/875ml milk
2oz./50g fresh yeast *or*
  2 tbsp./40ml dried yeast

6oz./150g caster sugar
3lb./1.5kg ordinary plain
  flour
½ tsp./2.5ml salt

Melt the margarine in the milk and allow to cool until lukewarm. Add the dried yeast and 1 tsp./5ml of the caster sugar and allow to froth *or* crumble in the fresh yeast. Sift the flour, remaining caster sugar and salt together. Make a well in the centre and pour in the yeast liquid. Mix until a dough is formed. Knead the dough until smooth and elastic. If kneading the mixture by hand, this will be a soft dough and should be kneaded on a well floured surface. Shape the dough into four 1lb. loaves, or rolls, plaits etc. (see page 15). Cover and prove until doubled in bulk. Bake at 400°F/200°C/Gas Mark 6, for 25–30 minutes for loaves, or 10–15 minutes for rolls. Cool on a wire rack.

CINNAMON ROLLS

1lb./400g sweet bread
  dough (see page 44)
2oz./50g butter, melted

1 tbsp./20ml brown sugar
2–3 tsp./10–15ml
  cinnamon

Roll out the dough to a 10 inch/25cm square, approximately ¼ inch/6mm thick. Brush the surface with melted butter, sprinkle over brown sugar and cinnamon. Roll up like a swiss roll and cut into slices ½ inch/12mm thick. Place cut side up on a baking sheet. Cover and allow to prove. Bake as for rolls. Cool on a wire rack.

Makes approximately 20 rolls.

RUM BABAS

Rum Babas are reputed to have been invented by a French Pastry Chef during the middle of the last century.

½oz./15g fresh yeast *or*
  2 tsp./10ml dried yeast
3 tbsp./60ml warm milk
4oz./100g strong plain
  flour
pinch of salt
½oz./15g caster sugar
2 eggs, beaten
2oz./50g butter, softened
2oz./50g currants

Syrup
4 tbsp./80ml golden syrup
4 tbsp./80ml water
2 tbsp./40ml rum

Lightly grease eight to ten 3½ inch/9cm ring tins with lard. Place the yeast, milk, and 1oz./25g of flour in a bowl and blend together, allow to froth for 15–20 minutes. Add the remaining flour, salt, sugar, eggs, currants and butter to the yeast mixture, and beat with a wooden spoon until smooth, for 2–3 minutes. Half fill the tins. Cover with a damp cloth and leave in a warm place to rise until the tins are two thirds full.

Bake at 400°F/200°C/Gas Mark 6 for 15–20 minutes. Meanwhile prepare the syrup, by heating the ingredients together. Bring to the boil and boil for 1 minute. Turn the babas out onto a plate. While they are still hot, spoon some of the syrup over each one until it has soaked through. Leave to cool.

If desired, serve the babas filled with whipped cream or fresh fruit salad.

Makes 8–10 babas.

HUTZELBROT

This is another bread from Germany, and the name means literally dried fruit bread.

½oz./15g fresh yeast *or*
  2 tsp./10ml dried yeast
  plus ½ tsp./2.5ml caster
  sugar
14fl.oz./350ml warm water
½ tsp./2.5ml salt
1½lb./600g ordinary plain
  flour
2oz./50g caster sugar
pinch of ground coriander
pinch of ground cloves
pinch of ground fennel
  seeds

2oz./50g dried apricots,
  chopped
1oz./25g dried apples,
  chopped
1oz./25g dried pears,
  chopped
4oz./100g whole hazelnuts
4oz./100g seedless raisins
3oz./75g chopped mixed
  peel
2oz./50g butter, melted

Froth the dried yeast with ½ tsp./2.5ml sugar in 5fl.oz./125ml of the warm water *or* crumble the fresh yeast in the same amount of liquid. Sift the flour, salt, sugar and spices together and add the fruit, nuts and peel. Add the remaining warm water to the frothed yeast liquid. Add the warm melted butter and yeast liquid to the dry ingredients and knead until the dough is smooth and elastic. Cover with a damp cloth and leave to rise in a warm place until doubled in bulk. This takes approximately 1½–2 hours.

Re-knead and divide the dough in two. Shape into rounds and place on a greased baking sheet. Allow the dough to prove for 30 minutes. Bake at 425°F/220°C/Gas Mark 7 for 15 minutes and reduce to 375°F/190°C/Gas Mark 5 for a further 15 minutes. Cool on a wire rack.

GERMAN PUMPERNICKEL

This recipe produces a light, fairly close textured pumpernickel

5oz./125g raw potato
½ pint/250ml water
2 tsp./10ml brown sugar
½oz./15g fresh yeast *or*
   2 tsp./10ml dried yeast
1oz./25g molasses
1oz./25g margarine

12oz./300g wholewheat
   flour
4oz./100g rye flour
2 tsp./10ml salt
1oz./25g bran
1oz./25g maize meal

Cook the peeled potato in boiling salted water until tender, drain and mash, allow to cool. Warm the water, add the brown sugar and yeast. If dried yeast is used allow to froth for 10–15 minutes. Warm the molasses and margarine gently over a very low heat. Sift the flours and salt together and mix in the bran, maize meal and potato. Make a well in the centre and pour in the yeast liquid, molasses and margarine. Gradually draw the dry ingredients into the liquid and mix until the dough comes cleanly away from the sides of the bowl.

Knead until smooth. Cover with a damp cloth and leave to rise in a warm place for 1½–2 hours or until doubled in bulk. Re-knead, and shape to fit a 2lb. loaf tin. Cover and leave to prove until risen to the top of the tin. Bake at 350°F/180°C/Gas Mark 4 for 45–50 minutes. Cool on a wire rack.

PRETZELS

These crisp, crunchy biscuits are delicious served with drinks or with cheese.

½oz./15g fresh yeast *or*
   2 tsp./10ml dried yeast
   plus ½ tsp./5ml caster
   sugar
½ pint/250ml warm water
1lb./400g strong plain
   flour
2 tsp./10ml salt
4 tsp./20ml caraway seeds

Glaze
1 egg, beaten
salt
caraway seeds

Froth the dried yeast and sugar in the warm water *or* crumble the fresh yeast in the warm water. Add the yeast mixture to the flour, salt and caraway seeds and mix to form a dough. Knead until smooth and elastic. Cover the dough with a damp cloth and leave for 45–60 minutes or until doubled in bulk. Re-knead. Divide into approximately 48 pieces. Roll each piece to an 8 inch/20cm long sausage shape. Place each piece on working surface, take the ends and curve towards you to make a semi-circle. Make a loop half-way along the curved side and twist once. Bring the ends back and twist them firmly onto the curve of the loop.

Half fill a large pan with boiling water and drop the pretzels into the boiling water. When they rise to the surface remove from the pan, drain and place on greased baking sheet. Brush with beaten egg and sprinkle with salt and caraway seeds. Bake at 375°F/190°C/Gas Mark 5 for approximately 25 minutes or until golden in colour. Eat the same day.
Makes approximately 48 pretzels.

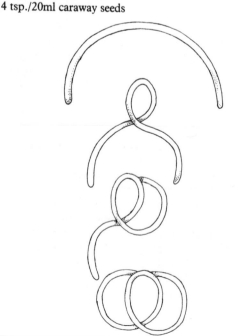

ALMOND TEA RING

Batter
¼oz./7.5g fresh yeast *or*
  1 tsp./5ml dried yeast
    plus ½ tsp./2.5ml sugar
4fl.oz./100ml warm milk
2oz./50g strong plain flour

Dough
1oz./25g margarine
6oz./150g strong plain
  flour
½ tsp./2.5ml salt
1 small egg

Variations:
Gala Tea Ring

Filling
1oz./25g walnuts
6 glacé cherries
1oz./25g seedless raisins
1oz./25g brown sugar
1 tsp./5ml ground
  cinnamon
½oz./15g butter, melted

Filling
2oz./50g sugar
2oz./50g ground almonds
few drops almond essence
1 egg white
½oz./15g butter, melted

Icing
3oz./75g icing sugar
1 tsp./5ml lemon juice
2 tsp./10ml water
  (approximately)
3–4 glacé cherries
angelica

Icing
3oz./75g icing sugar
1 tsp./5ml lemon juice
2 tsp./10ml water
  (approximately)
6 walnut halves
small strip angelica

Follow the method for the Almond Tea Ring.

Swedish Tea Ring

Filling
2oz./50g soft brown sugar
2 tsp./10ml mixed spice
½ oz./15g butter, melted

Icing
3oz./75g icing sugar
1 tbsp./20ml water
  (approximately)
3–4 glacé cherries
4 walnut halves

Follow the method for the
Almond Tea Ring.

Froth the yeast in the sugar and milk plus 2oz./50g flour for 20 minutes. Rub the margarine into the remaining flour. Add the yeast liquid together with the egg and beat until smooth. Cover with a damp cloth and leave in a warm place for 1 hour or until doubled in bulk.

Meanwhile prepare the filling by mixing the sugar, ground almonds and almond essence together, adding enough egg white to form a soft paste.

Roll the dough to a rectangle 8 × 14 inches/20 × 35cm. Brush with melted butter and spread filling over. Roll up tightly to form a long sausage. Place on a greased baking sheet and curve the ends round to form a ring and pinch the ends together to seal. Make cuts a half to three quarters way through the dough with scissors at an angle, about 1 inch/2.5cm apart. Fan out sections on their sides. Cover and prove for about 30–35 minutes. Bake at 375°F/190°C/Gas Mark 5 for 30–35 minutes. Cool on a wire rack.

To prepare icing sieve the icing sugar into a bowl. Add the lemon juice and sufficient water to make an icing of a fairly firm consistency. Spoon over the top of the baked, cooled tea ring and allow to run down the sides. Halve the cherries and cut the angelica into diamond shapes and decorate the tea ring before the icing sets.

EASTER BREAD

Dough
12oz./300g strong plain flour
½ tsp./2.5ml salt
½oz./15g fresh yeast *or*
  2 tsp./10ml dried yeast plus ½ tsp./2.5ml caster sugar
8fl.oz./200ml warm milk
1 tsp./5ml mixed spice

3oz./75g seedless raisins
3oz./75g sultanas
2oz./50g mixed peel
1oz./25g butter, softened

Almond Paste
3oz./75g ground almonds
1½oz./40g icing sugar
1½oz./40g caster sugar
½ tsp./2.5ml lemon juice
1 small egg, beaten
few drops almond essence

Follow the method for white bread (see page 18) adding the spice with the flour. Cover with a damp cloth and leave to rise in a warm place for 30 minutes or until doubled in bulk.

Re-knead, working in the dried fruit, peel and butter. Roll out to form an oblong the same length as a 2lb. loaf tin. Work all the ingredients of the almond paste together. Form the almond paste into a sausage shape and place on top of the dough. Mould the dough around the paste tucking in the join underneath. Place in the greased 2lb. loaf tin cover and leave to rise for 1 hour or until doubled in bulk. Brush with milk and bake at 425°F/220°C/Gas Mark 7, for 10 minutes, then at 350°F/180°C/Gas Mark 4 for a further 45 minutes. Cool on a wire rack and dredge with icing sugar when cold.

GREEK EASTER BREAD

This bread is served on Easter Saturday to celebrate the end of Lent. The loaf is sometimes decorated with bright red eggs, hardboiled in a solution of red food colouring and water.

1oz./25g fresh yeast *or*
  1 tbsp./20ml dried yeast plus ½ tsp./2.5ml caster sugar
5oz./125g caster sugar
½ pint/250ml warm milk
2lb./800g ordinary plain flour
1 tsp./5ml salt

3oz./75g chopped mixed peel
grated rind of 1 lemon
grated rind of 1 orange
6 egg yolks, beaten
1oz./25g butter melted
2–3oz./50–75g sesame seeds

1 egg yolk mixed with 1 tbsp./20ml cold water

Froth the dried yeast with ½ tsp./2.5ml caster sugar and the warm milk, *or* crumble the fresh yeast in the warm milk.

Put the flour, salt, remaining sugar, fruit rind and mixed peel into a bowl and mix together.

Add the melted butter to the yeast mixture with the beaten egg yolks. Add to the flour mixture and knead until smooth and elastic. Cover with a damp cloth and leave to rise in a warm place for 1–1½ hours until doubled in bulk.

Divide the dough into 3 equal pieces and roll each piece into a sausage shape approximately 12 inches/30cm long. Roll each piece in the sesame seeds and make a plait (see page 15). Place on a greased baking sheet, cover and leave to double in bulk for approximately 2 hours. Glaze the bread with the egg yolk mixed with water. Bake at 400°F/200°C/Gas Mark 6 for 10 minutes and reduce heat to 350°F/180°C/Gas Mark 4 for a further 30 minutes. Leave the bread to cool on the tray for half an hour and then remove to cooling rack.

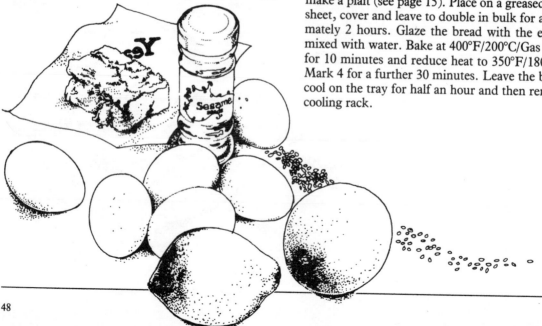

HUNGARIAN COFFEE CAKE

This cake is traditionally served with coffee.

Dough
1lb./400g strong plain
   flour
½oz./15g fresh yeast *or*
   2 tsp./10ml dried yeast
   plus 1 tsp./5ml caster
   sugar
8fl.oz./200ml warm milk
1 tsp./5ml salt
2oz./50g margarine
1 egg, beaten

Decoration
2oz./50g butter, melted
4oz./100g caster sugar
1 tsp./5ml ground
   cinnamon
1–2oz./25–50g chopped
   walnuts

Blend 5oz./125g of the flour, with the yeast, sugar and warm milk in a large bowl until smooth. Set aside for about 20 minutes or until frothy.

Sift the remaining flour with the salt and rub in the margarine. Add the beaten egg and flour mixture to the batter and mix well to give a fairly soft dough that leaves the sides of the bowl clean. Knead until it is no longer sticky. Put in a clean bowl cover with a damp cloth and leave to rise in a warm place for 1 hour or until doubled in size.

Divide the dough into 24 pieces of equal size and roll into balls the size of a walnut. Roll each ball in the melted butter. Mix the caster sugar, ground cinnamon and walnuts together and roll each ball of dough in this coating. Arrange them in a double row round a large oiled ring mould, leaving room for rising. Cover and prove for about 30 minutes. Bake at 400°F/ 200°C/Gas Mark 6 for 25–30 minutes. Cool on a wire rack.

CHAPATIS

Chapatis are a staple food for many Indian people, particularly the Punjabis. They are delicious served with or without butter. Keep hot by piling them up inside a dry teacloth. They are traditionally used to transfer food from dish to mouth.

8oz./200g ordinary plain
   flour or wholemeal flour
1 tsp./5ml salt
8fl.oz./200ml water,
   approximately

Place flour and salt in bowl, add water until a soft dough is formed. Knead until smooth. Leave dough in the bowl and cover with a damp cloth. Leave for at least 1 hour (the longer the dough stands the more pliable and digestible it becomes). Re-knead and divide into six pieces about the size of an apple. Flatten them with a rolling pin to about the size of a pancake. Cook in a lightly greased, heavy frying pan, for a few minutes on each side until lightly browned and puffy in the centre.
Makes 6 chapatis.

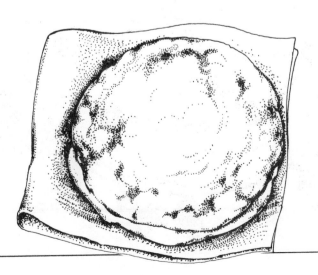

PLAIN PIZZA BASE

½oz./15g fresh yeast *or*
  2 tsp./10ml dried yeast
  plus ½ tsp./2.5ml caster
  sugar
¼ pint/125ml warm water

½oz./15g lard
1 tsp./5ml salt
8oz./200g ordinary plain
  flour

Follow the method for white bread (see page 18). Cover and put to rise in a warm place for 1 hour or until doubled in bulk. Either roll out the dough to a 12 inch/30cm circle or divide into four or six pieces and shape into rounds approximately 6 inches/15cm in diameter. Place on a greased baking sheet. The plain base does not need proving.

WHOLEMEAL PIZZA BASE

1oz./25g fresh yeast *or*
  1 tbsp./20ml dried yeast
  plus ½ tsp./2.5ml caster
  sugar

¼ pint/125ml warm water
8oz./200g wholemeal flour
½oz./15g lard
1 tsp./5ml salt

Follow the method for the plain base (see above). Cover and leave the dough in a warm place for 1 hour or until doubled in bulk. Knead and roll out to a 12 inch/30cm circle. Place on a greased baking sheet and prove for 30 minutes before topping.

To complete your plain or wholemeal pizza base, follow one of the following topping recipes.

Pizza Napolitana

1lb./400g tomatoes, skinned and sliced
salt and pepper
8oz./200g Mozzarella cheese, thinly sliced

2oz./50g anchovy fillets, drained
1 tsp./5ml dried oregano
black olives
olive oil

Arrange the sliced tomatoes on top of the dough (leaving ¼–½ inch/6–12mm around the edge) and season with salt and pepper. Arrange the thinly sliced cheese on the top. Cut the anchovies in half and arrange over the cheese. Decorate with the olives and sprinkle on the dried oregano. Sprinkle on some olive oil. Prove for 30 minutes. Bake at 425°F/220°C/Gas Mark 7 for 20–25 minutes for the large pizza or 10–15 minutes for the smaller ones. Serve hot.
Serves 4–6.

Pizza Francescana

1–2oz./25–50g butter
8oz./200g mushrooms, sliced
6oz./150g Bel Paese cheese
1lb./400g tomatoes, skinned and sliced
8oz./200g ham, cubed

salt and pepper
1tsp./5ml mixed herbs
2oz./50g anchovies, drained
1 clove garlic, crushed
olive oil

Fry the mushrooms in the butter. Crush the garlic and mix with the cheese and spread over the dough leaving approximately ½ inch/12mm around the edge. Arrange the mushrooms on top, then the ham and finally the tomatoes. Decorate with the anchovies. Sprinkle on herbs and olive oil. Prove for 30 minutes. Bake at 425°F/220°C/Gas Mark 7 for 20–25 minutes. Serve hot.
Serves 4–6.

Tuna Pizza

1lb./400g onions, thinly sliced
olive oil
1lb./400g tomatoes, skinned and sliced

2 × 6½oz./165g cans tuna fish, drained and flaked
14 capers
olives
salt and pepper
2oz./50g anchovies

Fry the onions in a little oil until lightly browned and then drain. Cover the pizza base with tomatoes. Spread over the flaked tuna fish, then onion rings, capers and olives. Season. Decorate with anchovies and sprinkle with oil. Prove for 30 minutes. Bake at 425°F/220°C/Gas Mark 7 for 20–25 minutes. Serve hot.
Serves 4–6.

CHALLAH

This is a Jewish egg bread.

½oz./15g fresh yeast *or*
    2 tsp./10ml dried yeast
2 tsp./10ml caster sugar
8fl.oz./200ml warm water
1lb./400g ordinary plain flour
1 tsp./5ml salt
2 eggs, beaten

Glaze
1 egg yolk, beaten together with 1 tbsp./20ml water
poppy seeds

Froth the dried yeast in the warm water together with ½ tsp./2.5ml of caster sugar *or* crumble the fresh yeast in the warm water. Add 6oz./150g of the flour to the yeast liquid and mix until well blended. Cover with damp cloth and leave for 1 hour or until doubled in bulk. Add the remaining flour, salt and sugar with the eggs to the risen dough and knead for 10 minutes. Cover with a damp cloth and leave in a warm place until doubled in bulk.

Re-knead the dough and divide into three equal pieces. Plait these to form a loaf. Moisten the ends with water and press them together. Place on a greased baking sheet. Cover with a damp cloth and leave in a warm place for 1 hour or until doubled in bulk. Brush with the glaze and sprinkle with poppy seeds.

Bake at 400°F/200°C/Gas Mark 6 for 10 minutes then at 375°F/190°C/Gas Mark 5 for 30 minutes. Cool on a wire rack.

KULICH – FESTIVE EASTER BREAD

In Russia this bread is traditionally cooked for the Orthodox Easter Celebrations. The bread should be cut horizontally in thin slices and the top replaced to prevent the loaf from drying out.

1½oz./40g fresh yeast *or*
   1½ tbsp./30ml dried
   yeast plus ½ tsp./2.5ml
   sugar
7fl.oz./175ml warm milk
3oz./75g raisins
3 tbsp./60ml rum
1½lb./600g ordinary plain
   flour
½ tsp./2.5ml salt
8oz./200g unsalted butter
9oz./225g icing sugar
9 egg yolks
¼ tsp./1ml saffron soaked
   in 1 tbsp./20ml hot
   water
½ tsp./2.5ml vanilla
   essence
2oz./50g flaked almonds
3oz./75g chopped mixed
   peel

Icing
6oz./150g icing sugar
1 tsp./5ml lemon juice
water to mix

Froth the dried yeast in the warm milk with the sugar *or* crumble the fresh yeast in the milk. Soak the raisins in the rum for 15 minutes. Sift flour into a bowl, rub in the butter, add the icing sugar and mix together. Make a well in the centre and pour in the yeast liquid together with the egg yolks, vanilla essence and saffron. Knead for 10–15 minutes until smooth and elastic. Cover with a damp cloth and leave to rise in a warm place for 1 hour or until the mixture doubles in bulk.

Toast the almonds under the grill, and add to the raisins with the mixed peel.

Grease a 2lb. coffee tin or tall cylindrical mould about 6 inches/15cm in diameter and 7 inches/18cm high. Line with greased greaseproof paper, allowing excess paper to come over the rim.

Add the fruit, nuts and peel to the mixture and re-knead. Place the dough in the tin and leave to rise in a warm place for approximately 45 minutes or until doubled in size. Bake at 400°F/200°C/Gas Mark 6 for 40 minutes and then turn to 350°F/180°C/Gas Mark 4 and bake for a further hour. Cool in the tin for 10 minutes and then remove onto a wire rack to cool completely.

Prepare the icing by sieving the icing sugar into a bowl; add the lemon juice and sufficient water to mix to a thick paste. Pour onto the top of the cake and allow to trickle down the sides. Leave to set.

RYE CRISPBREAD

This recipe comes from Sweden.

½oz./15g fresh yeast *or*
   2 tsp./10ml dried yeast
   plus 1 tsp./5ml sugar
6fl.oz./150ml warm water
   and milk
5oz./125g rye flour
5oz./125g plain white flour
pinch salt

½ tsp./2.5ml sugar
½ tbsp./10ml black treacle
1 tbsp./20ml oil
1oz./25g crushed
   cornflakes
1 tsp./5ml salt
½ tsp./2.5ml caraway
   seeds

Froth the yeast in milk and water with the sugar *or* crumble the fresh yeast into the liquid. Combine the dry ingredients. Make a well in the centre and pour in the yeast liquid, molasses and oil and mix until a dough is formed. Knead until smooth, cover with a damp cloth and leave in a warm place for 1 hour or until doubled in bulk. To the risen dough knead in the salt, crushed cornflakes and caraway seeds. Roll out thinly and cut into oblongs approximately 2½ × 5 inches/6 × 12.5cm. Place onto greased baking sheets. Leave to rise until slightly puffy. Bake at 400°F/200°C/Gas Mark 6 for 10–15 minutes until golden and crisp. Cool on a wire rack. Store in an airtight tin.
Makes approximately 16 crispbreads.

SWEDISH LIMPA BREAD

7fl.oz./175ml brown ale
1 tbsp./20ml caraway seeds
1 tbsp./20ml malt vinegar
4oz./100g black treacle
½oz./15g fresh yeast *or*
  2 tsp./10ml dried yeast

7oz./175g ordinary plain
  flour
8oz./200g rye flour
1 tsp./5ml salt
1oz./25g lard

Place the brown ale, caraway seeds, vinegar and treacle in a pan and heat until just warm (but not hot). Crumble in fresh yeast *or* add the dried yeast stirring until dissolved.

Combine the flours and salt in a bowl and rub in lard. Make a well in the centre and pour in the yeast liquid and knead until smooth and elastic. Return to bowl. Cover with a damp cloth and leave in a warm place for 45 minutes or until almost doubled in bulk. Re-knead for a second time. Shape into one round loaf or two batons. Place on a greased baking sheet, cover and prove for approximately 45–60 minutes.

Bake at 350°F/180°C/Gas Mark 4, for approximately 40 minutes. Cool on a wire rack.

SWISS BUNS

1oz./25g fresh yeast *or*
  1 tbsp./20ml dried yeast
  plus 1 tsp./5ml caster
  sugar
7fl.oz./175g warm milk
  and water
1lb./400g strong plain
  flour
1 tsp./5ml salt
2oz./50g caster sugar
2oz./50g lard, rubbed in
1 egg, beaten

Icing
10oz./250g icing sugar
2–3 tsp./40–60ml water

Combine the yeast, 1 tsp./20ml sugar, liquid and 4oz./100g flour together and leave to froth for 20–30 minutes. Mix together with the remaining ingredients. Knead dough until smooth and no longer sticky. Cover and leave in a warm place to double in bulk.

Divide into ten pieces and shape into 5 inch/12.5cm long pieces and roll up. Place rolls on a greased baking tray, cover and leave to prove. Bake at 425°F/220°C/Gas Mark 7 for approximately 15 minutes. Cool on a wire rack.

To prepare the icing mix the sugar and water together to form a coating consistency. When the buns are cool dip them into the glacé icing.
Makes 10 buns.

BROA

This is a corn bread from Portugal.

4oz./100g maize meal
½ tsp./2.5ml salt
6fl.oz./150ml boiling water
1 tbsp./20ml cooking oil

½oz./15g fresh yeast *or*
  2 tsp./10ml dried yeast
  plus 1 tsp./5ml sugar
3 tbsp./60ml warm water
8oz./200g ordinary plain
  flour

Blend 3oz./75g maize meal in a bowl with the salt. Stir in the boiling water and oil, and beat until the mixture is smooth. Leave to cool until lukewarm. In a bowl, froth the dried yeast with the warm water and sugar *or* crumble the fresh yeast in the warm liquid. Add yeast liquid to maize meal mixture together with the remaining maize meal and 3oz./75g of plain flour. Mix to form a soft dough and cover with a damp cloth and leave in a warm place for 1 hour or until doubled in bulk. Knead in the remaining flour to make a stiff dough. Brush an 8 inch/20cm sandwich tin lightly with oil. Place dough in tin and leave to double in bulk. Bake in the centre of the oven at 350°F/180°C/Gas Mark 4 for 45–50 minutes. Cool on a wire rack.

PASTRY

PASTRY

Shortcrust pastry is perhaps the most widely made of all the pastries. Once mastered it can be speedily made into pies, tarts, flans and pastries. Mothers on tight budgets with growing families can rely on short-crust pastry to help extend the more expensive fillings. However, at the same time do not lose sight of the fact that it is delicious in its own right. Success-ful shortcrust pastry should be crisp and light with no blemishes.

In all recipes using pastry the weight given always refers to the flour weight, in other words 8oz. short-crust pastry refers to pastry made with 8oz. flour.

General Proportions
To each 1lb./400g flour:
  1 tsp./5ml salt
  8oz./200g fat
  4–5 tbsp./80–100ml water

Notes on Ingredients

Flour
Plain flour gives the crispest texture; use a branded plain flour which is milled from softer varieties of wheat. Self-raising flour is preferred by some although it gives a texture that is softer, and more 'cake like'.

Any white flour should be sifted well to aerate it and remove any lumps. Wholemeal flour can be used in place of white flour although it may be necessary to add a little extra water to bind the mixture together. The texture of the pastry will depend on the brand of flour used. Home-milled flour will produce coarser pastry than branded flour. As the pastry is fairly dark in colour before baking, it will be necessary to time the length of cooking carefully rather than rely on the look as there is little change in the colour. If cooked for too long, wholemeal pastry becomes hard and rather nasty.

Fat
For everyday baking it is best to use equal quantities of margarine and lard. Margarine gives pastry colour and flavour, whilst lard improves the texture. For more special occasions butter can be used for extra flavour, or a mixture of butter and lard to give a shorter texture. Traditionally hard margarines have been used as they are more easily handled during rubbing in, but soft 'tub' margarines used straight from the refrigerator give successful results. Whipped vegetable shortening or oil may also be used.

Liquid
Water should be as cold as possible when added to the rubbed in mixture, and just enough used to bind the dough together without making it sticky. Wholemeal flour may absorb more water than white flour. For richer pastry an egg yolk or even a whole egg may be substituted for water. Allow approximately 1 tsp./5ml liquid to 1oz./25g flour.

Salt
Salt is essential to pastry to give it flavour.

Shortcrust Pastry
8oz./200g flour
4oz./100g fat
½ level tsp./5ml salt
2–3 tbsp./40–60ml cold
  water

The first rule for making shortcrust pastry is to keep everything – ingredients, utensils and hands – as cool as possible and handled as little as possible. The following basic method will ensure crisp light pastry rather than the tough chewy kind.

Sift the flour with the salt. Drop the fat into the flour cut into 1 inch/2.5cm cubes. Rub the fat into the flour, using your thumb along your fingertips. Keep your hands well above the mixture in order to aerate it; continue until the mixture resembles bread-crumbs.

If you wish to use a mixer, switch to the lowest speed to start with, increasing to a medium speed until the mixture resembles breadcrumbs. Take care not to overrub. You will know if this happens as the mixture will turn bright yellow and stick together.

Add the water and mix in with a round bladed knife until the pastry begins to draw together. If you are using a mixer, mix in the water at minimum speed until just incorporated. Again take care not to overmix. Draw the pastry mixture together with the fingertips to form a ball and knead lightly for a few seconds until perfectly smooth and even. Let the pastry 'rest' preferably in the refrigerator, while you prepare the filling. Roll out on a lightly floured board with a lightly floured rolling pin in short light movements away from you. Take care not to use too much flour as this will alter the consistency of the dough, jeopardizing the results.

Turn the pastry, not the rolling pin, to alter the shape and take care not to stretch the pastry or it will shrink in cooking. Roll to approximately ⅛ inch/3mm thickness and use as required.

Bake at 400°F/200°C/Gas Mark 6 for 15–20 minutes; if the filling needs longer cooking reduce the heat to 325°F/170°C/Gas Mark 3.

Shortcrust pastry is not normally glazed. Sweet dishes are usually dredged after cooking with caster or icing sugar. Sometimes savoury pies are brushed with beaten egg or milk, sweet pies with white of egg and caster sugar, before baking.

Variations
Cheese Pastry
8oz./200g plain flour
2oz./50g butter
2oz./50g finely grated, well
   flavoured cheese, e.g.
   Cheddar or Parmesan
   pinch salt, plus a pinch
   of dry mustard (if
   desired) beaten egg or
   water to bind

Mix in the cheese after the butter has been rubbed into the flour, but before the liquid is incorporated.

Pastry using Oil or Whipped Shortening
8oz./200g plain flour
8oz./200g whipped
   shortening *or*
   4 tbsp./80ml cooking oil
2½ tbsp./60 ml cold water

The method for this pastry differs slightly from conventional shortcrust pastry. Sift the flour with the salt. If mixing by hand place 2 heaped tbsp. of flour in the mixing bowl, make a well in the centre and pour in the oil and water or add the whipped shortening and water. Fork the mixture together until smooth and then incorporate the remainder of the flour. If using a mixer place the oil or fat and water into the bowl, add the flour and mix on the lowest speed until mixed together.

Knead and roll as usual; oil pastry is more suitable as a lining rather than covering as it tends to be soft. Bake as usual.

Flan Pastry
8oz./200g plain flour
6oz./150g butter
1 tsp./5ml caster sugar
1 egg, beaten

Method as for standard shortcrust pastry, adding the sugar and egg after the fat has been rubbed into the flour.

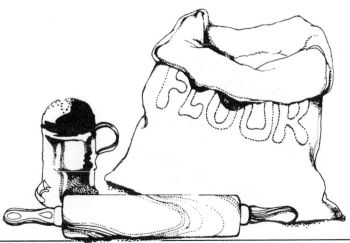

QUICHE LORRAINE

4oz./100g shortcrust pastry made with ordinary plain flour (see page 56)
3oz./75g lean bacon, chopped

4oz./100g gruyère cheese, thinly sliced
2 eggs
¼ pint/125ml single cream or creamy milk
salt and pepper

Line a 7 inch/18cm plain flan ring with the pastry. Cover the chopped bacon with boiling water and leave for 2–3 minutes, then drain well. Put the bacon into the pastry case with the cheese. In a basin beat the eggs, add the milk or cream and seasoning. Pour into the flan case. Bake at 400°F/200°C/Gas Mark 6 for approximately 30 minutes until set. Serve warm. *Serves 4–6.*

FRIED PEACH PIES

12oz./300g ordinary plain flour
pinch salt
5oz./125g margarine
6 tbsp./120ml water (approximately)

Filling
1lb./400g fresh peaches
2oz./50g sugar
1½ level tbsp./30ml cornflour
1 tsp./5ml lemon juice
pinch nutmeg
pinch cinnamon

caster sugar for sprinkling

Deep fat bath

Skin, stone and finely chop the peaches. Place the chopped peaches into a saucepan and add all the filling ingredients. Cook the mixture over a low heat, stirring constantly, until it boils gently and becomes thick and clear. Remove from heat and cool.

Make up the pastry by rubbing the margarine into flour and salt until it resembles breadcrumbs. Add sufficient water to form a stiff dough. On a lightly floured surface roll the pastry out thinly. Using a pastry cutter, cut into approximately thirty 3 inch/7cm circles.

Place some of the peach filling on one half of each circle. Damp the edge of the other half of the pastry with water. Fold the pastry over the filling and seal the edges together. Crimp with a fork.

Heat the oil to 190°C/375°F, place several pies in the frying basket and fry for about 4 minutes, until golden brown. Remove and drain. Sprinkle with caster sugar.
Makes approximately 30 pies.

CORNISH PASTIES

8oz./200g shortcrust
pastry, made with
ordinary plain flour *or*
4oz./100g wholemeal
and 4oz./100g plain
flour (see page 56)

Filling
8oz./200g lean chuck steak
1 medium sized potato
1 small carrot
1 medium sized onion
salt and pepper
1 egg, beaten with a little
milk

Divide the pastry into 4 pieces and roll each quarter into a circle 6½ inches/16.5cm in diameter. Chop the filling ingredients into ¼ inch/6mm dice and mix together. Divide the filling between the four circles, placing it down the middle. Brush the edges with water and draw up the pastry on each side of the filling in a line over the centre and seal firmly. Flute the edges.

Place the pasties on a greased baking sheet, brush each with beaten egg and milk. Bake in the centre of the oven at 425°F/220°C/Gas Mark 7 for 15 minutes, and then reduce to 325°F/170°C/Gas Mark 3 for a further hour. Serve warm.
Serves 4.

LEMON MERINGUE PIE

4oz./100g shortcrust
pastry, made with
ordinary plain flour (see
page 56)
½ pint/125ml water
4 level tbsp./80ml
cornflour
2 eggs, separated
2 medium sized lemons
(juice and zest)
6oz./150g caster sugar

Line a greased 7 inch/18cm plain flan ring with pastry. Line carefully with foil and bake blind for 15 minutes at 400°F/200°C/Gas Mark 6. Mix the water and cornflour in a saucepan, and bring to the boil. Cook for 2 minutes, stirring all the time.

Remove from heat and allow to cool slightly. Add the egg yolks, lemon rind, 4oz./100g sugar and lemon juice, beating well to form a smooth mixture. Pour into flan case.

Whisk egg whites until they are stiff and form peaks and fold in the remaining sugar lightly with a metal spoon. Spread on top of the lemon filling. Bake at 425°F/220°C/Gas Mark 7 for approximately 10 minutes until golden in colour. Serve hot or cold.
Serves 4–6.

ALMOND TARTLETS

This recipe uses an enriched pastry.

4oz./100g butter
3oz./75g caster sugar
1 egg yolk
3oz./75g ground almonds
9oz./220g ordinary plain
flour
4 tsp./20ml water
approximately
soft fruit or jam
½ pint/250ml double
cream, whipped

Cream butter and sugar together until pale, add egg yolk, almonds, flour and sufficient water to form a soft dough. Chill. Roll out on a lightly floured board and use to line 30 greased patty tins. Bake at 325°F/170°C/Gas Mark 3 for approximately 15–20 minutes until pale and golden. Cool in tins, and then remove to a wire rack. When cold fill with soft fruit or jam, and serve with whipped cream.
Makes approximately 30 tartlets.

PINEAPPLE AND RAISIN CHEESECAKE

8oz./200g ordinary plain
   flour
pinch salt
1 level tbsp./20ml ground
   ginger
4oz./100g butter
1½oz./40g caster sugar
1 egg yolk blended with
   approximately
     2 tbsp./40ml water

Filling
2oz./50g seedless raisins
8oz./200g can pineapple
   chunks, drained and
   chopped
8oz./200g cottage cheese
2 × 5oz./125g cartons
   soured cream
2oz./50g caster sugar
2 whole eggs plus 1 egg
   white
grated zest 1 lemon

Sift flour, salt and ginger into a bowl, rub in butter until the mixture resembles fine breadcrumbs. Add sugar and mix to a stiff dough with egg yolk and water. Wrap in foil and chill for 1 hour.

Roll out pastry thinly on a floured surface and line a 9 inch/22cm flan ring. Reserve pastry trimmings. Line carefully with foil and bake blind for 15 minutes at 400°F/200°C/Gas Mark 6. Remove foil and baking beans and bake for a further 5–10 minutes.

To make filling cover surface of pastry with raisins and pineapple. Blend together remaining ingredients and pour over the top of the fruit. Cook at 350°F/180°C/Gas Mark 4 for about 20–25 minutes until top is firm. Use pastry trimmings for a lattice of strips across top of pie and return to the oven for approximately 25 minutes until cooked. Allow to cool. Serve cold.
Serves 4–6.

WHOLEMEAL FRUIT CRUMBLE

This is not strictly speaking pastry, but a close enough relative to be included in this section. The addition of wholemeal flour gives a lovely 'nutty' flavour to this recipe.

4oz./100g margarine,
   cubed
8oz./200g wholemeal flour
2oz./50g sugar
1lb./400g prepared fruit,
   either canned or fresh

Rub the margarine into the flour until the mixture resembles fine breadcrumbs. Stir in the sugar. Grease a 2 pint/1 litre pie dish and fill with the prepared fruit. Press the crumble mix onto the top. Smooth and bake at 350°F/180°C/Gas Mark 4 for 35–45 minutes. This dish may be served hot or cold.
Serves 4–5.

BAKEWELL TART

6oz./150g shortcrust pastry, made with ordinary plain flour (see page 56)

Filling
4oz./100g butter
4oz./100g caster sugar
4oz./100g ground almonds
1 egg
3oz./75g ground rice
½ tsp./2.5ml vanilla essence
2 tbsp./40ml red jam
a little milk

Grease an 8 inch/20cm flan tin, line with pastry and reserve the pastry trimmings. Prepare the filling by heating butter until just melted. Stir in sugar and cook for 1 minute. Remove from heat and stir in ground almonds, egg, rice and vanilla essence. Spread jam over pastry base and pour on filling. Roll out pastry trimmings and cut into strips approximately ½ inch/12mm wide and arrange in a lattice shape over filling. Fix strips with a little milk.

Bake at 400°F/200°C/Gas Mark 6 for approximately 30 minutes until filling is well risen and golden brown. Remove from flan tin and cool on wire rack.
Serves 6.

LEEK AND ONION FLAN

4oz./100g shortcrust pastry made with ordinary plain flour (see page 56)
2 small leeks
1 large onion
1 clove garlic

2oz./50g butter
salt and black pepper
8fl.oz./200ml evaporated milk (unsweetened)
1 egg, beaten
2oz./50g cheese, grated

Line a greased 7 inch/18cm plain flan ring with pastry.

Trim the leeks and wash thoroughly to remove all grit and mud. Cut into ½ inch/1.5cm slices. Cut the onion into thin slices and crush the garlic. Cook the vegetables in the butter for approximately 5–10 minutes or until well softened. Season with salt and pepper and remove from heat. Mix the evaporated milk and egg together and stir in the vegetables and half the grated cheese. Pour the filling into the uncooked pastry case and sprinkle the remaining cheese on top. Bake at 350°F/180°C/Gas Mark 4 for 25–30 minutes or until pastry is cooked and filling set. Serve warm.
Serves 4–5.

APFEL STRUDEL

8oz./200g ordinary plain flour
½ tsp./2.5ml salt
1 egg, lightly beaten
2 tbsp./40ml cooking oil
4 tbsp./80ml lukewarm water
2½lb./1kg cooking apples, peeled, cored and thinly sliced

3oz./75g caster sugar
1½oz./40g seedless raisins
2oz./50g currants
1 tsp./5ml ground cinnamon
1½oz./40g melted butter
4oz./100g ground almonds

Sift flour and salt into a bowl. Make a well in centre, pour in the egg and oil, mix gradually adding the water to make a soft dough. Knead until smooth. Leave to rest for 1 hour. Mix together apples, sugar, raisins, currants and cinnamon.

Spread out a clean dry tea cloth onto a large working surface and sprinkle lightly with flour. Roll out the dough to a rectangle about ⅛ inch/3mm thick. Lift and turn to prevent the dough from sticking. Gently stretch the dough, working from the centre outwards using the backs of your hands, until it is paper thin. Trim to a rectangle 27 × 24 inches/67 × 60cm.

Arrange dough with one long side towards you, brush with melted butter and sprinkle with ground almonds. Spread over the filling leaving a 2 inch/5cm border around the edge. Fold pastry edges over the apple to contain filling. Lift corners of the cloth and roll up strudel like a Swiss Roll.

Place on a greased baking sheet, brush with melted butter and bake at 375°F/190°C/Gas Mark 5 for approximately 40 minutes. If necessary you can cut the strudel in half, folding the cut edges to enclose the filling.

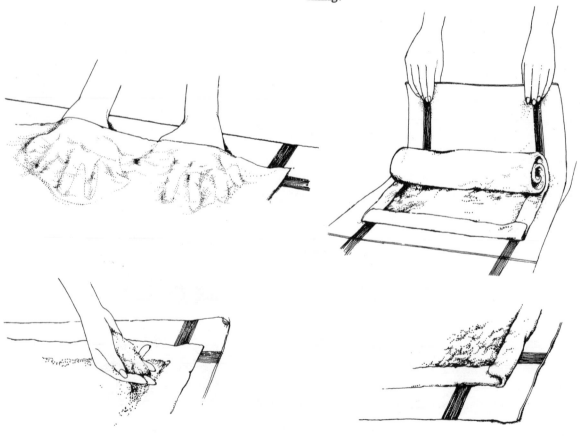

SUETCRUST PASTRY

Suetcrust is sadly becoming the Cinderella of pastries now that we are more diet conscious. Yet there is nothing to beat an old-fashioned steak and kidney pudding, brimming full of rich gravy and tender meat for comfort on frosty days. Sweet puddings made with fruit, syrup and jam are just as good and should not be overlooked.

Made well, suetcrust pastry should be light and airy, though it's too often wet and tough. It is cooked by either boiling or steaming for about 3 or 4 hours. This makes it ideal for dishes using cheaper cuts of meat. Serve meat pudding from the basin wrapped around in a colourful napkin. Turn sweet puddings out onto a dish.

General Proportions
To each 1lb./400g flour:
8oz./200g suet
5 tsp./25ml baking powder
2 tsp./10ml salt
½ pint/250ml water

Notes on Ingredients

Flour
A soft flour is used, preferably self-raising, as suet pastry needs a raising agent to give the light airy texture. If a plain flour is used it is necessary to add baking powder.

Wholemeal flour may be used successfully, using either all wholemeal or half white and half wholemeal. Suet pastry made entirely from wholemeal flour will have a closer texture.

Fat
Fat in the form of suet is incorporated into the flour. Beef suet is considered to be the best although it does require a certain amount of preparation. Skin and blood vessels should be removed and the suet grated on a coarse grater. Branded, ready-prepared suet is available from grocers and supermarkets; it saves trouble but is more expensive.

Liquid
A high proportion of water is required. The dough once mixed should be soft and elastic but not sticky.

Salt
Salt is essential for flavouring.

Basic Recipe
Cook either in a steamer or pan of boiling water, on top of the cooker. It is important that the water never comes off the boil or the pastry will become heavy and soggy.

4oz./100g fresh beef suet
or shredded suet
8oz./200g self raising flour
or plain with 2½
tsp./12.5ml baking
powder
¼ pint or 8 tbsp./125ml or
160ml water

Method
Prepare the suet as detailed above. Sift the flour with the baking powder and salt. Toss the suet in the flour and combine with knife or use a mixer on slow speed, until the mixture looks like coarse breadcrumbs. Make sure that the suet is well distributed throughout the flour. Add the water and continue cutting in or mixing until a soft elastic dough is formed. Knead lightly either using the mixer on a low speed or by hand on a floured board until smooth. Cover the dough in the mixing bowl and leave to 'rest' for 5–10 minutes before using.

Always steam or simmer puddings for at least 1½ hours. This length of time is needed to melt down the suet and so 'shorten' the pastry.

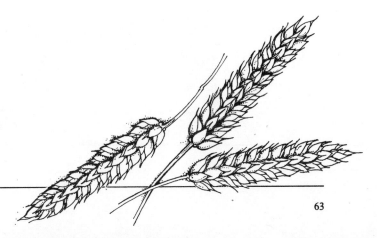

STEAK AND OYSTER PUDDING

12oz./300g suetcrust pastry
(see page 63)
8oz./200g ox kidney, cut
into 1 inch cubes
1lb.8oz./600g buttock or
chuck steak, cut into
cubes
1 small tin oysters
1 onion, finely chopped
1 clove garlic, peeled and
finely chopped
6oz./150g flat mushrooms
1oz./25g plain flour
salt and pepper
¼ pint/125ml beef stock
1 small glass sherry
1 tsp./5ml Worcestershire
Sauce

Grease a 2 pint/1 litre pudding basin. Roll the pastry into a circle large enough to fit the inside of the basin. Cut out a segment approximately one-third of the total, and set aside. Line the basin with the remaining two-thirds, sealing the join firmly.

Combine the steak, kidney, oysters, onion, garlic, mushrooms, flour and seasoning, and place into the lined basin. Pour over the stock, sherry, Worcestershire Sauce, and oyster liquid. Fold the edges of suet crust pastry over the meat. Roll the remaining one-third of the pastry into a lid to fit the basin, damp the outside of the lid and place on top of the meat in the basin. Press together. Cover the top with a lid of foil twisted in position and steam for 3½–4 hours. *Serves 4–6.*

MAKE the most of wheat by starting the day healthily as illustrated opposite. Sprinkle home-milled bran on muesli or using the basic ingredients of flour, yeast and water, bake your own french bread, wholemeal bread or croissants.

COMPLETE a traditional afternoon tea, as the top picture shows, with toasted crumpets, dripping with butter.

Fresh from the oven the danish pastries above make a delicious snack.

The picnic illustrated opposite is guaranteed to satisfy all healthy outdoor appetites: a raised meat pie, savoury quiche lorraine, fresh rolls, sandwiches and rich fruit cake.

1	Fruit buns	10	Currant bread
2	Flowerpot loaf	11	Rosemary bread
3	Farmhouse loaf	12	Hutzelbrot
4	Oatmeal rye bread	13	Cheese loaf
5	Apricot and walnut bread	14	Stollen
6	Wholemeal rice bread	15	Rye crisp-bread
7	Plait	16	Pitka
8	Soda bread	17	Oat and cara-way bread
9	Corn bread	18	Swedish Limpa

THE pastry case around the boeuf en croûte in the top picture ensures that none of the succulent meat juices are lost during cooking.

The crêpes suzettes above are featherlight pancakes, flamed in brandy: a sophisticated dish that never fails to impress.

Savarin, gâteau St. Honoré, profiteroles, cream slices, brandy snaps, the mouthwatering puddings opposite illustrate flour's versatility in dough, pastry and biscuit recipes.

STEAK AND KIDNEY STEW WITH DUMPLINGS

2 large onions
8oz./200g carrots
1–1½lb./400–600g stewing
   steak
½lb./200g kidney,
   trimmed
1oz./25g plain flour
2 tbsp./40ml oil
1½ pints/750ml hot beef
   stock
bouquet garni (bay leaf,
   thyme, peppercorns,
   parsley)
salt and pepper

Dumplings
6oz./150g self raising flour
   (or if desired 3oz./75g
   wholemeal flour,
   1 tsp./5ml baking
   powder, 3oz./75g self
   raising flour)
3oz./75g prepared suet
5–6 tbsp./100–120ml water

Chop the onions and slice the carrots. Cut the meat and kidney into even sized cubes, and toss in flour. Heat the oil in a large pan, cook the onions until golden, add the meat and brown on all sides. Add the carrots, stock, bouquet garni and seasoning and bring to the boil. Simmer for 1½–2 hours until the meat is tender and the carrots cooked. Meanwhile prepare the dumplings: follow method for suet crust on page 63, roll the dough into balls, and add to the casserole. Continue simmering the stew for 20–30 minutes. Remove the *bouquet garni* and correct seasoning before serving.
Serves 5–6.

GOLDEN LAYER PUDDING

8oz./200g suetcrust pastry
   (see page 63)

10–12oz./250–300g golden
   syrup
2oz./50g breadcrumbs

Grease a 1½–2 pint/¾ litre pudding basin, divide the pastry into 4 pieces, roll out one piece into a circle to fit the bottom of the basin. Cover it with syrup and sprinkle with breadcrumbs. Repeat the layering, finishing the top with a layer of pastry. Lightly dust with flour, cover with foil and stand in boiling water and simmer steadily for 2 hours. Refill with boiling water if necessary. Serve hot.
Serves 4–6.

APPLE AND CINNAMON ROLL OR JAM ROLY-POLY

This is a delicious way to serve apples, but you can make an economical variation by using 8oz./200g jam instead of the fruit filling.

8oz./200g suetcrust pastry
   (see page 63)

Filling
1lb./400g cooking apples
2oz./50g sultanas
2 tsp./10ml cinnamon
2oz./50g caster sugar

Wash, peel and slice apples, mix with the sultanas, cinnamon and sugar. Roll out dough on floured surface to a rectangle which will fit your largest pan. If necessary it can be curled round the edge of the pan. Spread over the filling to within ½ inch/12mm of edges. Turn in the edges to contain the filling and brush them with water. Roll up the pastry from the longest side to form a sausage shape. Enclose in foil, sealing well. Put into a pan of boiling water, bring back to the boil and boil for about 1½ hours. Remove foil, place on a serving dish, dredge with caster sugar.
Serves 4–6.

P REPARE your own pasta dough, with plain or wholemeal flour, cut into thin strips for fettucine or tiny shapes for minestrone soup. Top a bread dough with tomatoes, olives and anchovies for an appetizing pizza.

HOT WATER CRUST PASTRY

This very robust pastry is made by mixing together boiling water, melted lard and flour. It is moulded by hand, either pressed into a hinged mould, loose bottomed cake tin or shaped around the bottom of a jam jar. This type of pastry is only used for meat, particularly game, pies which are often highly decorative.

During cooking the meat will settle within the pie crust leaving a space between it and the pastry; traditionally this space is filled with melted jelly poured through a hole in the top and allowed to set; this 'finishes' the pie making it more attractive when cut.

Hot water crust should be crisp and firm and, together with a tasty filling, makes a handsome meal.

General Proportions
To each 1lb./400g flour:
4oz./100g lard
2 tsp./10ml salt
¼ pint plus 4 tbsp./150ml
 plus 60ml liquid

Basic Recipe
8oz./200g plain flour
2oz./50g lard
1 tsp./5ml salt
⅛ pint/75ml plus 2
 tbsp./40ml water

Notes on Ingredients

Flour
A plain general purpose flour is suitable for this pastry, half wholemeal may be substituted if desired.

Fat
Lard is always used and this is melted in the water. An egg yolk may be added for extra flavour and colour. The white may be used to brush the inside of the pie before filling.

Liquid
Boiling water is commonly used, although milk or milk and water may be substituted.

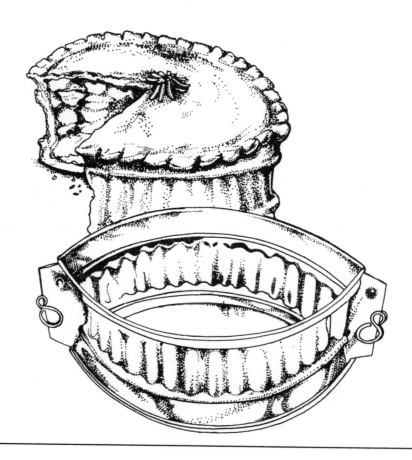

Method

Sift the flour with the salt. Place lard and liquid in a saucepan and heat gently until the lard has melted. Increase heat and bring to the boil. Pour the boiling liquid into the flour and mix until smooth with a wooden spoon or an electric mixer on low speed. Use your hands to knead it if a mixer is not available. Shape the dough into a ball, cover and rest in a warm place for 20–30 minutes. The cooking time and temperature depend upon the recipe.

To raise hot water crust pies without a hinged pie mould

1. Choose a suitable sized jar or cannister and dredge liberally with flour.
2. Prepare the pastry.
3. Using two-thirds of pastry, roll out a circle double the diameter of the jar or cannister. For example, if using a 4 inch/10cm diameter jar roll 8 inch/20cm circle. Keep rest of pastry covered.
4. Lift the pastry with the rolling pin and transfer to the upturned jar.
5. Shape the pastry pressing firmly to the sides of the jar.
6. Put a piece of greaseproof paper round the pie and hold it in position with string.
7. Rest the pastry in a cool place until firm.
8. Ease the mould carefully from the pastry case, twisting at first to loosen.
9. Pack in filling firmly, especially at the sides to help pie keep its shape.
10. Roll out the remaining pastry to fit the top of the pie.
11. Brush the edges with beaten egg or water.
12. Fit the top to the pie, and press edges together to seal. Trim away surplus pastry from the edges, and remove greaseproof paper.
13. Make two slits crosswise at the top, fold back the pastry pieces to form a small hole.
14. Make some decorative leaves with any trimmings to fit the hole.
15. Brush pie well with beaten egg glaze.

INDIVIDUAL RAISED PORK PIES

8oz./200g hot water crust
    pastry (see page 66)
1lb.4oz./500g boneless
    pork
½ pint/250ml chicken
    stock
1 tbsp./20ml parsley,
    chopped
Salt and pepper
1 egg, beaten with a pinch
    of salt to glaze

Jelly
¼ pint/125ml hot stock or
    water
½ level tsp./2.5ml gelatine
Salt and pepper

Prepare the hot water crust while the meat is cooking.

Cut the meat into approximately ½ inch/12mm cubes; put into a pan with chicken stock and simmer for approximately 1 hour until tender.

Drain the meat reserving stock and leave to cool. When cool mix the meat with salt and pepper, add the parsley.

Divide the pastry into four pieces. Using well floured jars approximately 2½ inches/6cm in diameter, make four pastry cases about 2 inches/5cm high, reserving one-third of each portion of pastry for lids. Rest the pastry in a cool place until firm. Remove from the jars and place on a greased baking sheet.

Divide the meat filling into four, and fill each pastry case, packing the meat in tightly. Add approximately 1 tsp./5ml of reserved stock to each pie.

Roll out the remaining pastry and make lids, cutting them slightly larger than the pies. Brush the edges with beaten egg, put on the lids and bring up the edges above the meat and flute. Cut a small hole in the lid to allow for the steam to escape. Brush with beaten egg.

Bake at 400°F/200°C/Gas Mark 6 for 30–40 minutes until pastry is cooked crisp and brown. Allow to cool.

Dissolve gelatine in stock or water, season and allow to cool until setting point is reached. With a funnel, fill the cavities in the pies with jelly and allow to set firmly.

Makes 4 pies.

RAISED VEAL AND EGG PIE

8oz./200g hot water crust
    pastry (see page 66)
1lb./400g pie veal
4oz./100g bacon, chopped
1 tbsp./20ml chopped
    parsley
rind and juice of 1 lemon
pinch thyme
salt and pepper
little stock
1 egg, hard boiled
1 egg, beaten with a pinch
    of salt to glaze

Jelly
¼ pint/125ml hot stock *or*
    water
½ level tsp./2.5ml gelatine
salt and pepper

Using two-thirds of the pastry to mould the case around an 8oz./200g coffee jar approximately 4 inches/10cm diameter (see page 67).

While the pastry is resting cut the veal into ½ inch/12 mm cubes, add parsley, lemon, thyme, seasoning and a little stock to moisten. Put half the filling into the pastry case, place the egg in the middle and cover with the remaining filling. Brush the edges with the beaten egg; roll out final third as a lid, seal edges cut a vent in the middle and decorate. Brush with beaten egg.

Bake at 425°F/220°C/Gas Mark 7 for 15–20 minutes, then at 350°F/180°C/Gas Mark 4 for 1½ hours; allow to cool. Prepare jelly and fill pie cavity as described in recipe above.

Serves 6.

GAME PIE

8oz./200g hot water crust pastry (see page 66)
meat from 1 cooked pheasant, chopped
8oz./200g boneless pork, chopped
6oz./150g chuck steak, chopped
salt and pepper
1 egg, beaten with a pinch of salt to glaze

Jelly
½ pint/250ml stock or water
1 level tsp./5ml gelatine
salt and pepper

Shape the pie case by moulding two-thirds of the pastry around a floured jar with a base 4 inches/10cm in diameter. Rest the pastry in a cool place until firm. Remove from jar and place on a baking sheet; fill with the meat and seasonings. Brush edge of pie with beaten egg or water and put on the lid, made from remaining third of pastry, seal and flute edges. (If a thicker pastry crust is desired use 12oz./300g of flour made into hot water crust.) Brush lid with beaten egg and pinch salt. Make a fairly large hole in the centre of the pie about 1 inch/2.5cm. Decorate with pastry trimmings and bake at 425°F/220°C/Gas Mark 7 for 15–20 minutes, then at 350°F/180°C/Gas Mark 4 for a further 1½ hours. Allow to cool.

Dissolve the gelatine in the water or stock, season and allow to cool until setting point is reached. Using a funnel fill the pie with the jelly and allow to set. *Serves 6*.

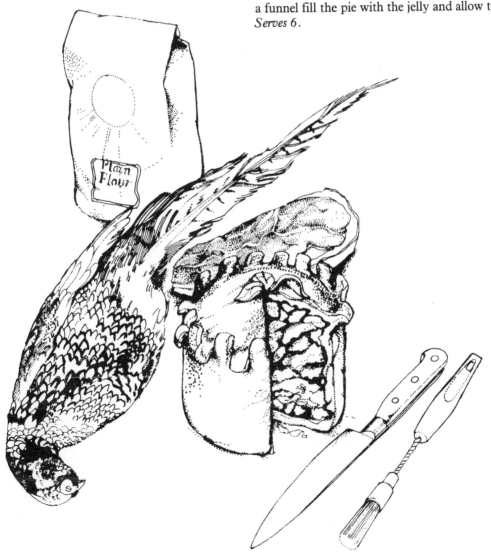

FLAKY-TYPE PASTRIES

There are three types of 'flaked' pastries – flaky pastry, rough puff pastry and puff pastry.

All three comprise paper thin layers of pastry with air trapped in between. Well made 'flaked' pastry should keep a good shape and have light even flakes. Flaky and rough puff pastry are very similar and may be interchanged. The difference between them lies in the method of adding the fat and it is really only personal preference that dictates which is used. Puff pastry is the richest of the three and requires more time and patience to be made successfully.

Nowadays ready-made frozen puff pastry is frequently used to replace home-made puff pastry. If a recipe calls for 8oz./200g quantity buy a 16oz./400g packet. Frozen pastry should be rolled out slightly thinner than home-made – to about the thickness of a small coin.

General Proportions for Flaky and Rough Puff Pastry
To each 1lb./400g flour:
- 12oz./300g fat
- ½ tsp./2.5ml salt
- 4 tsp./20ml lemon juice
- ½ pint/250ml water

General Proportions for Puff Pastry
To each 1lb./400g flour:
- 1lb./400g butter
- ½ tsp./2.5ml salt
- 4 tsp./20ml lemon juice
- 16 tbsp./320ml cold water

Basic Recipe for Flaky and Rough Puff Pastry
8oz./200g plain flour
6oz./150g fat – usually
  1–2oz./25–50g lard and
  4–5oz./100–125g
  margarine
pinch salt
2tsp./10ml lemon juice
¼ pint/125ml water,
  approximately

Basic Recipe for Puff Pastry
8oz./200g plain flour
8oz./200g unsalted butter
2 tsp./10ml lemon juice
pinch salt
8 tbsp./160ml cold water

Notes on Ingredients

Flour
Plain flour is always used for this type of pastry. Strong plain flour is preferable as it will give a stronger dough, although perfectly acceptable results can be obtained with ordinary household plain flour.

Fat
A mixture of butter or margarine and lard gives colour, flavour and lightness to flaky and rough puff pastry. Cost will determine which you use. For the richer puff pastry, butter is more suitable.

Liquid
Water, the colder the better, is always used. It helps if the water is iced.

Lemon Juice
The acid in lemon juice helps to strengthen the gluten in the flour, helping to give a good light flaky result.

General Points to Note for all Types
1. Always handle pastry lightly and as little as possible.
2. The fat for rough puff pastry should be firm, i.e. straight from the refrigerator so that the cubes of fat retain their shape during mixing.
3. Fat for flaky and puff pastries should be 'worked' on a plate first to soften. The fat should be the same consistency as the dough to which it is added.
4. Roll out evenly and lightly taking care not to stretch the pastry. Stretched pastry will make the finished dish go out of shape.

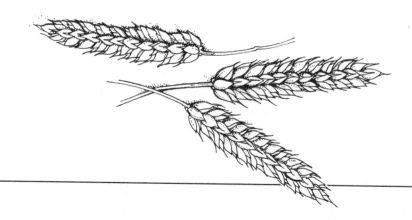

Method for Flaky Pastry

Sift the flour and salt together. Soften the fat by 'working' it with a knife on a plate. Divide into four equal portions. Rub a quarter of the fat into the flour, and mix to a soft dough with the water and lemon juice. Use a knife or a mixer on low to medium speed.

On a lightly floured board roll out a rectangle three times as long as it is wide. Using the end of a round bladed knife, transfer another quarter of fat over the top two-thirds of the strip in small pats. Fold the bottom third up over the fat and the top third down over that. Turn through 90 degrees so that the folds are at the side. Seal the edges by pressing together with your hand. Re-roll as before and continue until all the fat is used up. Wrap in foil and leave to rest in the refrigerator for at least half an hour before using. This firms the fat and makes handling and shaping simple as well as giving a more even texture.

The usual cooking temperature for flaky pastry is 425°F/220°C/Gas Mark 7.

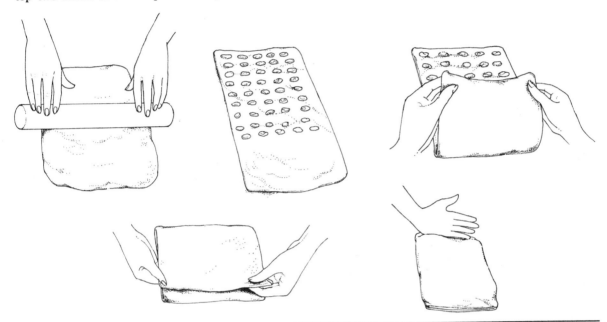

Method for Rough Puff Pastry

Sift the flour and salt together. Using the fat straight from the refrigerator, cut into ½ inch/12mm cubes and drop into the flour. Add the lemon juice and water. Mix with a round bladed knife, taking care not to break up the pieces of fat.

Turn onto a lightly floured board and roll into a rectangle three times as long as it is wide. Fold the bottom third up and the top third down over the pastry. Turn through 90 degrees so that the folds are at the sides, seal the edges of the pastry by pressing together with a rolling pin. Continue the rolling and folding four times over. Wrap in foil and leave to rest in the refrigerator for at least half an hour before using. This firms the fat and makes handling and shaping simpler.

The usual cooking temperature for rough puff pastry is 425°F/220°C/Gas Mark 7.

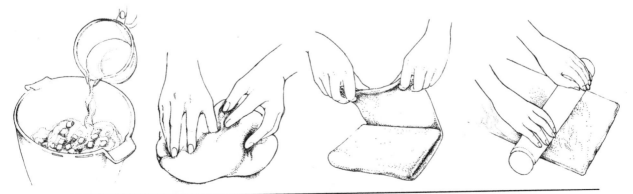

Method for making Puff Pastry

Sift the flour and salt. Soften the fat by 'working' it with a knife on a plate. Add a knob of fat to the flour and rub in. Mix in the water and lemon juice to form a soft elastic dough, either with a knife or a mixer on low to medium speed. Place dough on a lightly floured board, and roll out into a square. Form the remainder of the fat into a block. Place the block on one half of the pastry and enclose it by folding the pastry over and sealing the edges with a rolling pin. Turn the pastry so that the fold is to the side and roll out into a rectangle three times as long as it is wide. Fold the bottom third up and the top third down over it. Seal the edges by pressing lightly with a rolling pin. Wrap the pastry in foil and leave to rest in the refrigerator for about half an hour. Remove the pastry from the refrigerator turn it so that the fold is at the side and continue rolling, folding, and resting until the sequence has been completed six times altogether. After the final rest shape as required. The top surfaces of puff pastry are always brushed with beaten egg.

The usual cooking temperature is 450°F/230°C/Gas Mark 8.

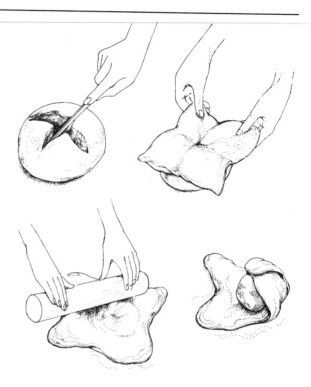

CHICKEN AND MUSHROOM PIE

1 small onion
4oz./100g streaky bacon
3lb./1.5kg chicken, jointed
4oz./100g whole
   mushrooms, wiped

¼ pint/125ml stock
salt and pepper
12oz./300g flaky pastry
   (see page 70)
1 egg, beaten

Finely chop the onion and bacon, arrange with the chicken and mushrooms in a 1½ pint pie dish and add the stock and seasoning. Roll out the pastry to an oval 2 inches/5cm larger than the pie dish. Cut off a strip 1 inch/2.5cm wide all round and fit onto rim of dish, pressing down well. Brush with water, transfer the remaining pastry on the rolling pin to the pie and press the edges down. Knock-up, i.e. use a knife to make a series of shallow cuts around the pastry edges. Lastly flute the edges by making a series of indentations between thumb and forefinger with the back of a knife. Brush the top with beaten egg. Allow to rest for 30–40 minutes. Brush the top once more with egg and bake 425°F/220°C/Gas Mark 7 for 25 minutes. Reduce heat to 325°F/170°C/Gas Mark 3 for a further 35 minutes. Serve hot.
Serves 4–6.

BOEUF EN CROÛTE

8oz./200g rough puff
  pastry (see page 70)
1 tbsp./15ml oil
3–3½lb./1.4–1.5kg topside
  of beef

Stuffing
1–2oz./25–50g butter
2 small onions, finely
  chopped
4oz./100g mushrooms,
  chopped
2 tbsp./40ml chopped
  parsley
salt and pepper

Glaze
1 egg, beaten

Pre-heat the oven 400°F/200°C/Gas Mark 6. Prepare the meat by heating the oil in a large pan, add the beef and fry the outside surfaces to seal in the juices. Transfer meat and oil to oven and roast for 15 minutes per 1lb./400g. Trim off any excess fat, and allow to cool. This will produce meat which is rare, so if desired roast for slightly longer.

To prepare the stuffing melt the butter in a pan, add the onion and fry until softened. Add the mushrooms, parsley and seasoning and cook for a further minute.

Roll out the pastry to a rectangle large enough to cover meat. Spread one third of the stuffing over centre of pastry and place the beef on top. Spread the rest of the stuffing around the meat. Dampen the edges of pastry and fold up over the meat like a parcel, trimming off excess pastry at each end. Reserve the trimmings. Turn meat over so that the pastry join is underneath and place in a greased roasting tin. Roll out the pastry trimmings and cut into leaves to decorate the top. Brush with beaten egg or milk. Increase the oven temperature to 425°F/220°C/Gas Mark 7 and cook beef for 40–45 minutes until pastry is crisp and golden brown. Remove to serving dish and garnish with watercress or parsley.
Serves 8.

RUSSIAN FISH PIE

½oz./15g butter
1½ tbsp./30ml flour
¼ pint/125ml milk
6oz./150g flaked, cooked,
  smoked haddock

1 tbsp./20ml parsley,
  chopped
seasoning
8oz./200g puff pastry (see
  page 70)
1 egg, beaten

Melt the butter in a pan, add the flour to form a roux stirring all the time. Remove pan from heat and slowly add milk, beating constantly. Return to heat, and cook, stirring, until the sauce comes to the boil and thickens. Remove from heat and add haddock and parsley. Season to taste. Allow to cool slightly.

Roll out the pastry to a square, approximately 10 × 10 inches/25 × 25cm. Place the filling in the middle; draw up the sides of the pastry and fold in the corners to form an envelope shape. Seal the edges. Brush with beaten egg and bake at 400°F/200°C/Gas Mark 6 for 30–35 minutes.
Serves 4.

TURKISH BOREKS

Filling
1 tbsp./20ml oil
1 medium onion, finely
  chopped
1 large green pepper,
  chopped
1lb./400g raw minced beef
1 heaped tbsp./20ml
  tomato purée
2 tbsp./40ml chopped
  parsley
salt and pepper
2 tsp./10ml Worcestershire
  sauce

1lb./400g puff pastry (see
  page 70)
1 egg, beaten
sesame seeds (optional)

Heat the oil and fry onion and pepper gently until golden, then add the minced meat and stir until the meat changes colour. Add the tomato purée, parsley and seasoning; cover and simmer for 15 minutes; a little more water or tomato purée may be added, but the mixture should be moist not wet. Allow to cool.

Roll out the pastry to the thickness of a penny and cut into 4 inch/10cm circles. Divide the filling between the circles, brush the edges with beaten egg, fold, seal, and crimp the edges. Brush with beaten egg, prick with a fork and sprinkle with sesame seeds if desired. Bake at 450°F/230°C/Gas Mark 8 for 15 minutes.
Makes 32–34 boreks.

ANCHOVY STICKS

8oz./200g puff pastry (see
  page 70)
1 tbsp./20ml grated
  parmesan cheese
1 tbsp./20ml cream or top
  of the milk

1 tbsp./20ml fresh white
  breadcrumbs
1 tbsp./20ml anchovy
  essence
1 egg, beaten

Roll out the pastry to a rectangle 18 × 6 inches/45 × 15cm, trim the edges and cut in half lengthwise. Mix the cheese, cream, breadcrumbs and anchovy essence to a firm paste. (Add a few extra breadcrumbs if the filling is too runny.) Spread the filling over one half of the pastry and cover with the second piece. Brush the top with beaten egg or milk. Cut into strips 1 inch/2.5cm wide.

Put on a damp baking sheet and allow to rest for 10 minutes. Bake at 425°F/220°C/Gas Mark 7 for approximately 20 minutes, until golden.
Makes approximately 18 sticks.

CHESTNUT LAYER GÂTEAU

8oz./200g flaky pastry (see
  page 70)
8oz./200g unsweetened
  chestnut purée
½ pint/250ml double
  cream

4oz./100g plain chocolate,
  melted in a basin over a
  pan of hot water
2oz./50g icing sugar,
  sieved

Roll out pastry thinly and cut into three 8 inch/20cm circles in diameter. Transfer onto a baking sheet, brushed with water; prick and bake at 425°F/220°C/Gas Mark 7 for approximately 15 minutes, until golden. Allow to cool.

Beat together the sugar, chestnut purée and 2oz./50g of the chocolate. Whisk in the double cream until the mixture is thick and forms soft peaks.

Trim the pastry circles to an even size, spread with most of the chestnut mixture and sandwich together. Cover the last pastry circle with the remaining chocolate and place on top of the others. Decorate with the remaining cream and serve as soon as possible.

CREAM SLICES

4oz./100g flaky or puff
  pastry (see page 70) *or*
8oz./200g frozen puff
  pastry
6 tsp./30 ml red jam
¼ pint/125ml double
  cream, whipped

Roll out the pastry to a rectangle 4 × 12 inches/10 × 30cm. Brush a baking sheet with water, lay the pastry on it. With a sharp knife cut the pastry into six rectangles 2 × 4 inches/5 × 10cm, but do not separate them. Bake at 450°F/230°C/Gas Mark 8 for about 10 minutes; separate the strips and cool. Split each strip in half and spread with a teaspoon of jam. Cover with whipped cream, replace the lid and dust lightly with icing sugar.

GÂTEAU PITHIVIERS

Filling
2oz./50g butter, melted
2oz./50g caster sugar
2oz./50g ground almonds
1 egg
1 tbsp./20ml flour
few drops almond essence
2 tbsp./40ml apricot jam

8oz./200g puff pastry (see
  page 70) *or* 1lb./400g
  frozen puff pastry

Glaze
1 egg, beaten

Mix the filling ingredients together until smooth omitting the apricot jam. Roll out the pastry into two circles (9 inches/22.5cm in diameter) one ⅛ inch/3mm thick, the other approximately ¼ inch/6mm thick.

Place the thinner circle on a baking sheet and spread over the jam to within ½ inch/12mm of the edge. Spread the almond mixture on top of the jam. Brush the edge with beaten egg (glaze ingredients). Place on the lid, pressing the edges together. Brush the top with egg and make arcs with a knife across the top. Make a small slit in the top to allow the steam to escape. Allow to rest for 5–10 minutes in a cool place. Using a knife, nick the edge of the pastry 12 times at regular intervals. Push up the pastry on either side of each nick to form a scalloped, rose petal edge. Bake at 450°F/230°C/Gas Mark 8 for 10–15 minutes, reduce to 375°F/190°C/Gas Mark 5 for 10 minutes. Cool on a wire rack.
Serves 6.

ECCLES CAKES

8oz./200g flaky pastry (see
  page 70)

Filling
1oz./25g butter or
  margarine
4oz./100g currants
1oz./25g mixed peel

1oz./25g brown sugar
½ tsp./2.5ml ground
  nutmeg

Topping
egg white
caster sugar

Melt the butter in a saucepan. Add the remaining filling ingredients and allow the mixture to cool.

Roll out the flaky pastry on a lightly floured surface. Roll out to approximately ⅛ inch/3mm thick and using a lightly floured cutter or knife cut out 5 inch/13cm rounds. Place 2 tsp./10ml of the filling in the centre of each round. Brush the edges of the pastry with water and then gather the edges together over the filling and seal well. Turn over the cakes and using a lightly floured rolling pin press into 3½ inch/8cm circles.

Rinse a baking sheet in cold water and shake to remove any excess water. Place the eccles cakes on the tray and using a floured knife make three slits across the top of each cake. Brush with egg white and sprinkle liberally with caster sugar. Bake at 425°F/220°C/Gas Mark 7 for 15–20 minutes or until golden brown.
Makes approximately 8–10 eccles cakes.

FRUIT JALOUSIE

12oz./300g puff pastry (see page 70)
1–1¼lb./400–500g plums *or* 2lb./800g frozen plums, thawed
2oz./50g caster sugar
1 egg, beaten

Wash and dry fresh plums. Halve and stone plums. Divide the pastry into two pieces, one slightly larger than the other. Roll out two rectangles, approximately 12 × 9 inches/30 × 22.5cm, making one thicker than the other.

Place the thinner rectangle on the baking sheet; fold the thicker one in half lengthwise and make a series of cuts every ¼–½ inch/6–12mm, starting ½ inch/12mm down from the top of the pastry, cutting straight through the folded edge. The cuts should come no closer than 1 inch/2.5cm to the sides. Unfold.

Put the plums on the pastry base to within 1 inch/2.5cm of the edge, sprinkle with caster sugar, and brush the edges with beaten egg. Lift the cut pastry top onto the plums, seal the edges and knock up. Brush with beaten egg.

Bake at 400°F/200°C/Gas Mark 6 for 20–30 minutes and serve immediately.
Serves 4–6.

PALMIERS

This is a good way of using up left over pieces of puff pastry.

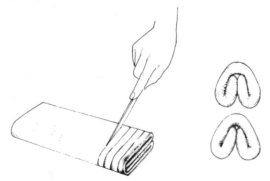

Roll out the pastry into a thin rectangle, and sprinkle with caster sugar. Fold the ends to the centre until they meet and press down firmly. Sprinkle generously with more sugar and fold the ends to the centre again, press and sprinkle with sugar. Place the two folded portions together and press. Cut into ¼ inch/6mm slices. Place cut edge down on a greased baking sheet allowing room for them to spread and bake at 425°F/220°C/Gas Mark 7 for approximately 6 minutes, turn over and bake the other side for further 6 minutes, and cool.

The palmiers can be sandwiched together with jam or cream.

CHOUX PASTRY

The high proportion of liquid in this pastry turns to steam during cooking, giving it an extremely light and puffy texture. Choux, (pronounced 'Shoo'); is French for cabbage and the pastry takes its name from the cabbage-like way in which it grows and bursts open. For good results the ingredients must always be measured accurately and each egg beaten in thoroughly to introduce the most important ingredient – air. This pastry is not rolled but piped on to a sheet or baking tin; cooking will cause it to rise and puff out with a natural cavity in the centre which may be filled in a variety of ways.

Basic Recipe
To each 2½oz./65g flour:
2oz./50g butter
¼ pint/125ml water
2 small eggs (sizes 6 and 7)
pinch of sugar or salt
    according to filling

Notes on Ingredients
A plain general purpose flour is suitable for Choux pastry. There are some schools of thought that say strong plain flour is superior, but the extra cost of strong flour is not really justified here.

Fat
Butter is used in this basic recipe as the flavour is superior. You may, of course, substitute margarine on grounds of economy.

Liquid
Usually water, although milk may be used.

Eggs
It is important to use small eggs to keep the mixture stiff. If the eggs are large in size a floppy paste will lead to disappointing results.

Method
Have ready a greased baking tray, forcing bag and plain pipe. Weigh and measure the ingredients carefully. Melt the fat with the salt/sugar in the liquid over a low heat. Bring to the boil.

Remove pan from the heat, add the flour and beat in vigorously with a wooden spoon until the paste forms a ball and leaves the sides of the saucepan clean. Beat in the eggs a little at a time vigorously with a wooden spoon. An electric mixer may be used at this stage; use a medium speed. The mixture should be smooth and glossy and stiff enough to stand in peaks if drawn up with the spoon. It is now ready to use.

Cream puffs or éclairs are cooked in a pre-heated oven at 400°F/200°C/Gas Mark 6. The oven door must not be opened during cooking.

During cooling, éclairs and profiteroles must be slit along their sides to allow the steam to escape and prevent the pastry becoming soggy.

PROFITEROLES

choux pastry using
    2½oz./65g flour (see above)
½ pint/250ml double cream, whipped

Chocolate Sauce
1oz./25g cocoa powder
1oz./25g caster sugar
1oz./25g margarine
2 tbsp./40ml water

Using ½ inch/12mm plain nozzle, pipe small balls of pastry about the size of a walnut onto lightly greased baking sheets. Bake at 425°F/220°C/Gas Mark 7 for 15–20 minutes until crisp. Remove from tray and prick to allow steam to escape. Cool on a wire rack.

Make a hole in the bottom of each profiterole and fill with whipped cream. Dust the profiteroles with icing sugar, and pile into a pyramid.

Make the chocolate sauce by heating all the ingredients together until the butter has melted, stirring all the time.

Pour the sauce over the profiteroles, or serve the chocolate sauce separately.

GÂTEAU ST. HONORÉ

4oz./100g shortcrust pastry, made with plain flour (see page 56)

3oz./75g choux pastry (see page 77)

Cream Patisserie
1½oz./40g butter
1½oz./40g flour
8fl.oz./200ml milk
2oz./50g caster sugar
2 egg yolks
¼ pint/125ml single cream

Caramel
4 tbsp./80ml water
4 tbsp./80ml caster sugar
1–1½lb./400–600g can peaches, drained
6 glacé cherries

Make up the shortcrust pastry and roll out to an 8 inch/20cm circle approximately ¼ inch/6mm thick. Put onto a greased baking sheet. Brush a ½ inch/12mm band around the edge with beaten egg. Make up the choux pastry and with a piping bag fitted with a ½ inch/12mm plain nozzle, pipe a circle of choux around the edge of the shortcrust pastry and brush it with beaten egg. Pipe the remaining choux pastry in small buns about the size of a walnut onto the baking sheet. Brush these with beaten egg. Bake both the flan and choux buns at 375°F/190°C/Gas Mark 5 for about 35 minutes or until well risen and browned. Prick the choux pastry at the base to allow for steam to escape. Cool.

For the pastry cream filling, make a roux by melting the butter gently and stirring in the flour off the heat. Pour in the milk and blend. Heat gently, stirring constantly, until a thick white sauce is formed. Add the sugar and allow to cool slightly. Mix the egg yolks with the cream, add to the white sauce and cook for 5 minutes. Allow to cool.

Fill a piping bag, fitted with a small nozzle, with the pastry cream. Make a small slit in the base of the choux buns, and remove any soft pastry; fill with some of the cream.

Reserve some of the peaches for decoration. Chop the remainder and add to the cream.

Dissolve the sugar in the water and bring to the boil. Boil until the edges just begin to darken. Dip the tops of the choux buns in the caramel using a skewer or fork to hold them. Use the remainder of the syrup to stick the buns on the choux pastry border. Fill the centre with the pastry cream mixture. Decorate with the peaches and cherries.

Serves 4–6.

ECLAIRS

choux pastry using
  2½oz./65g flour (see
  page 77)
½ pint/250ml double
  cream, whipped

Chocolate Icing
3oz./75g plain chocolate
8oz./200g icing sugar
2 tbsp./40ml hot water

Using a plain round ½ inch/12mm pipe force the
choux pastry onto a greased baking sheet, making
fingers approximately 3½ inches/9cm long. Bake in a
hot oven 400°F/200°C/Gas Mark 6 for approximately
30 minutes until well risen, golden and crisp. Slit each
éclair down the side to allow steam to escape, and cool
on a wire rack.

When cold, fill with whipped cream. Prepare the
icing by melting the chocolate in a basin over a pan of
hot, *not* boiling, water. Sieve icing sugar into a bowl,
add hot water and stir until well mixed. Add melted
chocolate and beat until smooth and shiny. The icing
should cling thickly to the back of a wooden spoon.
More hot water or icing sugar can be added to obtain
the proper consistency.

Carefully cover the tops of the éclairs with the
icing, using the back of a spoon to spread.
Makes approximately 14 éclairs.

SWEET BEIGNETS

choux pastry using
  2½oz./65g flour (see
  page 77)
3–4oz./75–100ml caster
  sugar
deep fat bath for frying

Apricot Sauce
4oz./100g apricot jam
¼ pint/125ml water
2 tsp./10ml cornflour or
  arrowroot

Heat the fat to 190°C or until small cube of day-old
bread immediately bubbles and browns when
dropped into the fat.

Drop small spoonsful of the choux mixture into hot
fat and cook for 7–8 minutes, turning occasionally.
Remove and drain, coat with caster sugar.

For the sauce, boil the water and jam, stirring
continuously. Blend the arrowroot or cornflour with
3 tsp./15ml water, add the jam mix stirring continuously. Rinse the pan, strain the mixture into it
and bring to the boil. Serve with the beignets.
Serves 4.

CHEESE AIGRETTES

choux pastry using
  2½oz./65g flour (see
  page 77)
1–2oz/25–50g grated
  cheese
salt and pepper
deep fat bath for frying

Make up the choux pastry, adding seasoning and
grated cheese.

Heat the oil to 190°C or until a small cube of
day-old bread immediately bubbles and browns when
dropped into fat.

Put the choux pastry into a piping bag fitted with a
½ inch/12mm plain nozzle, and pipe 1½ inch/4cm
lengths of pastry into the hot fat. Fry for 4–5 minutes,
or until golden. Drain and serve.
Serves 4–6.

CAKES & BISCUITS

CAKES & BISCUITS

Cakes and biscuits are the mainstay of the Great British afternoon tea. However, they are just as commonly used now to fill lunchboxes, feed hungry kids coming in from school, for desserts or just for a quick snack.

Commercially baked cakes and biscuits are numerous and readily available, but they are a totally different and certainly a less palatable alternative to the real, home-made thing. As long as you have an oven and mixing bowl, you will be able to make and bake something worthwhile. Ingredients like 'soft' margarines have helped much in home-baking. With this you can make cakes by the 'one-stage' method, surely the simplest yet.

Kitchen appliances such as food mixers and blenders take all the drudgery out of cake-making leaving you time to concentrate on the more skilful aspects without aching arms and stiff hands from clutching the wooden spoon.

Also available are cake mixes that you make up from ingredients in a package and bake yourself. They are useful in certain circumstances, but cakes and biscuits that are completely home-made are hard to beat.

TYPES OF CAKES

Cakes are divided into groups according to the method of mixing and the proportion of ingredients.

1. Rubbed-in Method
Here the fat is cut up in the flour and rubbed in with the fingertips until the mixture resembles fine breadcrumbs. This method is only suitable for recipes with half, or less than half, fat to flour.

2. Melting Method
The fat is melted with the sugar in recipes with either golden syrup or treacle. This particular method is generally used for gingerbread.

3. Creaming Method
The fat and sugar are creamed together until light and fluffy. This is suitable for recipes with half, or more than half, fat to flour.

4. Whisking Method
The eggs and sugar are whisked together either in a pre-warmed bowl or over a pan of hot water. The proportion of eggs and sugar is high in relation to the quantity of flour.

5. One-stage Method
All the ingredients are placed in the bowl and beaten together for 1–2 minutes. This method relies on the use of a commercially whipped or hydrogenated margarine, i.e. the type available in tubs, together with extra raising agent to compensate for the lack of manual aeration.

Raising Agents
Cakes and similar mixtures can be 'lifted' physically, mechanically or chemically to give the desired lightness and texture.

Physical
The physical way is to use the liquid present in prepared mixtures as steam. Here, a high proportion of liquid is needed together with a high baking temperature to make it effective. The texture of any mixture risen by steam is open and rather uneven.

Mechanical
Air can be introduced in a variety of ways; by sieving the flour, creaming, beating and whisking. After the introduction of air by one of these methods, prepared

mixtures should be treated with care and baked as soon as possible to avoid needless loss of air.

Chemical

Bicarbonate of soda, cream of tartar and the raising agent present in self-raising flour all produce carbon dioxide, which escapes through the crumb and crust of the mixture during cooking and is replaced with air. Normally bicarbonate of soda and cream of tarter are used together; if bicarbonate of soda is used on its own, say in scones, it will give an unpleasant after taste and dark yellow colour. Bicarbonate of soda can be used on its own in dark coloured, strongly flavoured mixes such as gingerbread or chocolate cake.

The constituents of 'baking powder' vary from brand to brand but all manufacturers have agreed that their brands shall release the same proportion of carbon dioxide; in other words, the same proportion of baking powder to flour may be used regardless of brand. Use 2½ tsp./12.5ml baking powder to 8oz./200g plain flour. Self-raising flour is a soft flour with a combination of raising agents evenly distributed throughout.

Flour

A soft flour with a low gluten content is best for cakes and biscuits. This type of flour absorbs fat well and gives a fine, light, close texture. For biscuits and shortbread, when no rise is needed, extra starch can be added to improve the texture. This can take the form of cornflour, rice flour, or even custard powder. Use 7oz./175g plain flour with 1oz./25g cornflour, rice flour, or custard powder and follow the basic recipe.

Whether you use self-raising flour or plain flour with a raising agent is a matter of personal choice. Self-raising flour is probably the most convenient to use and you can be sure of consistent results.

Wholemeal flour can be used to introduce variety. All types of wholemeal flour give a closer texture and nutty flavour. A mixture of half white and half wholemeal flour will add interest to the texture and flavour without being too heavy. It is a good idea to use this half-and-half mixture if you are not used to baking with wholemeal flour.

Fats

Block margarine and butter are the most commonly used fats. They are best used at room temperature, rather than straight from the refrigerator. Butter gives a better flavour and is vital for shortbread. 'Tub' or 'soft' margarines are best used straight from the refrigerator and are especially suited to 'one-stage' recipes. Other fats such as lard, blended white vegetable fat, oil and dripping are occasionally used.

Sugar

Caster sugar is the best to use in cake-making. Its fineness makes it especially suitable for creamed and whisked mixtures. Granulated sugar can be used, but there will be some reduction in volume and texture together with grittiness and speckling. Soft brown sugar, with its delicious caramel flavour, may also be used with a high degree of success. Demerara sugar is fine for cakes made by the melting method, but not so good for creaming as the sugar crystals do not break down. Barbados sugar, ideal for dark fruit cakes and gingerbread, has a very strong flavour resembling black treacle, which would be inappropriate in light cake mixtures.

Eggs

The eggs used in all the recipes in this section have been size 4 (standard), but larger eggs will give similar results. However, if smaller ones are used a slight adjustment will be necessary, i.e. for every three eggs specified one extra will be required.

Liquid

Liquid is required to combine ingredients and make steam to help the cakes to rise.

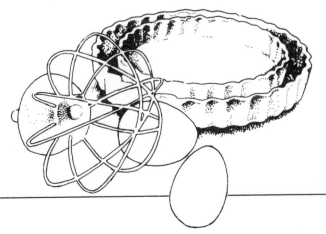

MELTED CAKE

Gingerbread (see page 98) and Parkin fall into this category.

8oz./200g ordinary plain flour
1 level tsp./5ml bicarbonate of soda
3oz./75g margarine
2oz./50g brown sugar

6oz./150g black treacle and golden syrup, mixed
3–4fl.oz./100–125ml milk
4oz./100g dried fruit (optional)
1½ tsp./7.5ml ground ginger

Weigh the ingredients, pre-heat the oven to 325°F/170°C/Gas Mark 3, grease and line the tins. Sift the dry ingredients into a bowl. Melt the sugar, syrup, treacle and margarine together, taking care not to boil. Cool.

Make a well in the centre of the dry ingredients and pour in the melted mixture. Beat either with a mixer *or* wooden spoon to form a smooth batter. Pour into the prepared cake tins. Bake slowly for approximately ¾–1 hour. Cool on a wire rack. The texture and flavour are improved if the gingerbread is stored in an airtight tin, or wrapped in foil, for a week before serving.

RUBBED-IN CAKE

8oz./200g ordinary plain flour
2–2½ tsp./10–12ml baking powder
3–4oz./75–100g margarine

3–4oz./75–100g granulated sugar
1 egg, optional
⅛–¼ pint/70–125ml milk
flavouring, e.g. grated orange or lemon rind, dried fruit etc.

Weigh the ingredients, pre-heat the oven to 400°F/200°C/Gas Mark 6, grease and line the tins.

Sift all the dry ingredients (not fruit) together, add the sugar. If mixing by hand, cut the fat into cubes and rub into the flour with the fingertips, until the mixture looks like coarse breadcrumbs. Add any flavouring. Beat the egg (if used) with the milk. Make a well in the dry ingredients and pour in the egg and milk and mix to a stiff consistency: the mixture should only fall from the spoon if it is shaken hard. *Or* if using a mixer, cut the fat into cubes and combine with the flour, using a low speed until the mixture resembles breadcrumbs. Take care not to over-mix. Add any flavouring specified. Still using a slow speed, fold the egg (if used) and milk and combine thoroughly to form a stiff mixture.

Transfer the mixture to a prepared tin and bake until well-risen and golden brown. Buns on trays are normally cooked at 400°F/200°C/Gas Mark 6 for 15–20 minutes. Larger cakes are cooked at around 350°F/180°C/Gas Mark 4 for about 1 hour, depending on size.

Cool on a wire rack.

CREAMED CAKES

This basic recipe can be varied according to the type of cake required. Perhaps the best known is the Victoria Sponge Sandwich.

4oz./100g self-raising flour
4oz./100g margarine
4oz./100g caster sugar
2 eggs

Weigh the ingredients, pre-heat the oven to 350°F/180°C/Gas Mark 4. Grease and line the tins. Make sure all ingredients are at room temperature before you begin and on colder days it is a good idea to warm the mixing bowl.

Sift the dry ingredients together. If mixing by hand, cream the fat and sugar together by beating with a wooden spoon until the mixture is white and fluffy looking, rather like stiffly whipped cream. Add any flavourings specified. Add the eggs one by one, beating in thoroughly. The mixture will curdle if this is not done properly. If that happens add 1 tbsp./10ml flour and continue. Sift the flour and fold into the mixture with a metal spoon. Add any fruit or liquid specified. *Or* if using a machine combine the margarine and sugar using a low speed. When the ingredients have come together increase the speed until the mixture is light and fluffy. Add any flavourings specified. Add the eggs one at a time on the maximum speed. Stop the machine from time to time and scrape down the mixture from the sides of the bowl to ensure thorough mixing. Sift in the flour and fold in using a low speed. Repeat this procedure with any liquid or fruit specified. Switch off the machine as soon as the ingredients have been incorporated to prevent the cake becoming tough through over-mixing.

Pour into the prepared tins and bake for 15–20 minutes. The temperature may vary according to the recipe, but it is normally a medium to slow oven, rather than a hot one.

ONE-STAGE CAKE-MAKING

This is the most modern method of cake-making brought about by the introduction of 'hydrogenated' fats. These are fats, processed to make creaming and general incorporation with other ingredients much simpler. With the 'one-stage' method of cake-making all the ingredients are placed into the mixing bowl and beaten for 2 minutes and then cooked. Both self-raising flour and baking powder are used to compensate for the lack of manual aeration. The ingredients should be used at room temperature.

4oz./100g self-raising flour
1 level tsp./5ml baking
   powder
4oz./100g caster sugar
4oz./100g tub of soft
   margarine
2 eggs
2 tbsp./40ml liquid (milk,
   fruit juice etc.)

Weigh the ingredients, pre-heat the oven to 350°F/180°C/Gas Mark 4, grease and line the tins. Sift the dry ingredients together.

Place all the ingredients in the mixing bowl and beat well for 2 minutes. The mixture should be smooth. Over- mixing will result in a tough cake.

If using an electric mixer, mix just long enough to incorporate the ingredients.

Place the mixture into prepared cake tins and bake for 20–25 minutes. Cool on a wire rack.

WHISKED CAKES

2oz./50g ordinary plain
  flour
2oz./50g caster sugar
2 eggs
few drops of vanilla
  essence

Weigh the ingredients, pre-heat the oven to 350°F/180°C/Gas Mark 4, grease and line the tins. Place the eggs and sugar into a heat-proof bowl. Set the bowl on a saucepan, one quarter filled with boiling water. Keep the pan on a low heat, taking care not to let the water come into contact with the bottom of the basin. Using a hand whisk or electric mixer, whisk the eggs and sugar together until pale in colour and thick enough to leave a trail behind the whisk. If using a table mixer, whisk the eggs and sugar together in the pre-warmed bowl on maximum speed.

Remove the bowl from the pan and sift the flour on top of the mixture. Carefully fold in with a metal spoon, using a cutting motion.

Note: the addition of flour must be carried out by hand even if you have previously whisked the eggs and sugar by machine.

Transfer the mixture to the prepared tin and bake immediately for 15–20 minutes approximately. Cool the cake on a wire rack.

WALNUT DATE LOAF

8oz./200g dates
14fl.oz./350ml boiling
  water
1½lb./600g ordinary plain
  flour
1 tsp./5ml salt

6oz./150g margarine
1lb./400g sugar
1 tsp./5ml bicarbonate of
  soda
6oz./150g walnuts

Stone dates and chop roughly, cover with boiling water. Sift flour and salt into bowl. Rub the margarine into the flour. Add the sugar and mix well.

Drain the water from the dates and reserve. Dissolve the bicarbonate of soda in the reserved water and add to the dry ingredients together with the eggs. Mix together well. Add the coarsely chopped dates and nuts.

Turn into three well greased 1lb./400g loaf tins. Bake in a slow oven 325°F/170°C/Gas Mark 3 for about 1½ hours. Cool on a wire rack.

Serve thinly sliced and spread with butter.

CHERRY SHORTCAKE

2oz./50g semolina
8oz./200g self-raising flour
5oz./125g margarine
4oz./100g caster sugar
4oz./100g glacé cherries,
  quartered

2 eggs, lightly beaten
1 tsp./5ml almond essence
2–3 tbsp./40–60ml milk

Mix the flour and semolina together. Rub the margarine into the flour until it resembles fine breadcrumbs. Add sugar and cherries to the mixture. Add the eggs and almond essence. Mix to a smooth consistency. Add sufficient milk to make a soft dropping consistency when the mixture drops from a spoon without shaking. Turn into a greased and lined 7 inch/17.5cm round cake tin. Bake 350°F/180°C/Gas Mark 4 for 1 hour approximately. Cut into pieces and allow to cool in the tin.

ALMOND BUNS

6oz./150g ordinary plain
  flour
pinch salt
½ tsp./2.5ml baking
  powder
3oz./75g margarine
1oz./25g caster sugar
1 egg, beaten

Almond Paste
2oz./50g ground almonds
1oz./25g caster sugar
1oz./25g icing sugar
few drops almond essence
1 small egg, beaten
Flaked almonds to
  decorate

Sift flour, salt and baking powder together, rub in margarine until it resembles breadcrumbs. Add sugar and bind into a paste with egg to make a smooth elastic dough. Make almond paste by mixing all the ingredients together and divide into 16 pieces.

Divide dough into 16 and flatten each piece. Place a ball of almond paste in middle of each piece and draw up the dough round the paste and mould into buns. Brush with beaten egg and sprinkle on the flaked almonds. Bake at 450°F/230°C/Gas Mark 8 for approximately 15 minutes.
Makes 16 buns.

ROCK CAKES

8oz./200g self-raising flour
4oz./100g margarine
pinch salt

3oz./75g caster sugar
4oz./100g dried fruit
1 egg, beaten
a little milk

Rub fat into flour and salt, add sugar and fruit, add the egg and sufficient milk to mix to a stiff dough.

Using two forks, place the mixture in rough heaps on a greased baking sheet and cook in centre of the oven at 400°F/200°C/Gas Mark 6 for 15–20 minutes or until golden brown. Cool on a wire rack.
Makes approximately 10–12 cakes.

For wholemeal rock cakes substitute 4oz./100g of wholemeal flour plus 4oz./100g of ordinary plain flour plus 1½ tsp./7.5ml of baking powder for the self-raising flour.

VICTORIA SANDWICH CAKE

4oz./100g butter or
  margarine
4oz./100g caster sugar
2 eggs

4oz./100g self-raising flour
2 tbsp./40ml jam
caster sugar to dredge

Grease two 7 inch/18cm sandwich tins and line the base of each with greaseproof paper. Cream the fat and sugar until pale and fluffy. Add the eggs one at a time, beating well after each addition. Fold in the flour with a metal spoon.

Place half the mixture in each tin and smooth the tops with a palette knife. Bake both cakes on the same shelf of the oven at 375°F/190°C/Gas Mark 5 for about 20 minutes, or until they are well-risen, golden, firm to the touch and beginning to shrink away from the sides of the tins. Turn out and cool on a wire rack.

When the cakes are cool, sandwich them together with jam and sprinkle the top with caster sugar.

The following variations can be made to the basic recipe:

Chocolate
Replace 3 level tbsp./60ml of flour with 3 tbsp./60ml of cocoa. For a moister cake blend the cocoa with water to give a thick paste, and beat into the creamed ingredients. Sandwich together with vanilla or chocolate butter cream (see page 88).

Orange or Lemon
Add the finely grated rind of one orange or lemon to the mixture. Sandwich the cakes together with orange or lemon curd or orange or lemon butter cream (see page 88). Use some of the juice from the fruit to make glacé icing (see page 96).

Coffee
Add 2 tsp./10ml instant coffee dissolved in a little warm water to the creamed mixture with the egg. Or use 2 tsp./10ml coffee essence.

WHOLEMEAL VICTORIA SANDWICH

4oz./100g margarine
4oz./100g caster sugar
2 eggs
6oz./150g wholemeal flour

1½ tsp./7.5ml baking
    powder
1 tbsp./20ml milk

Warm the mixing bowl while weighing out the ingredients. Cream the margarine and sugar together until pale and fluffy. Beat in the eggs one at a time beating until smooth. Add a spoonful of flour with the second egg. Fold in the flour, baking powder and milk together. Transfer to two greased and lined 6 inch/15cm sandwich tins and bake for 30–35 minutes at 375°F/190°C/Gas Mark 5. Cool on a wire rack.

The following variations can be made to the basic recipe:

Vanilla
Add ½ tsp./2.5ml vanilla essence when creaming the butter and sugar.

Orange or Lemon
Add 1 tsp./5ml of finely grated rind when creaming the butter and sugar.

Coffee
Add 1 tbsp./20ml strong black coffee in place of milk.

Chocolate
Sieve 1 tbsp./20ml cocoa powder with the flour and baking powder.

RABBIT CAKE

4oz./100g margarine
4oz./100g caster sugar
2 eggs
4oz./100g self-raising flour
    minus 3 tbsp.
3 tbsp./60ml cocoa powder

Icing
6oz./150g unsalted butter
12oz./300g icing sugar
few drops vanilla essence
milk
cocoa powder

To decorate
1oz./25g almond nibs
pink food colouring
2 chocolate buttons

Make up the chocolate victoria sandwich mixture (see page 87) sifting the cocoa powder with the flour. Bake in two 6½ inch/16.5cm greased sandwich tins. Cool on a wire rack.

Cream butter, icing sugar and vanilla essence to make very soft butter icing, adding a little milk if necessary.

Assemble the rabbit by cutting a circle 4 inches/10cm in diameter out of one cake for the head. Cut the remaining sponge into eight equal pieces. Follow the drawing below and join the pieces together to make four feet. Cut a 4 inch/10cm square out of the other cake to form the body. Following the drawing join the sponge pieces into two ears.

Join the pieces of cake together with a little butter icing. Reserve approximately 1 tbsp./20ml of butter icing and colour with a little cocoa powder.

Cover the rabbit completely with the remaining plain butter icing. Rough up with a fork.

Colour the almond nibs by dipping in some pink food colouring and water.

Put some of the almond nibs on paws. Use the chocolate buttons for eyes and then with chocolate butter icing pipe nose, mouth and whiskers.

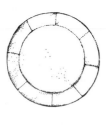
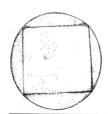

PINEAPPLE UPSIDE-DOWN PUDDING

1 quantity of victoria
sandwich mixture (see
page 87)
1 tbsp. /20ml golden syrup

8fl.oz./225ml can
pineapple rings
glacé cherries

Make up the victoria sandwich mixture. Grease a 2
pint/1 litre ovenproof dish and spread golden syrup
evenly over the bottom. Drain the can of pineapple
rings. Arrange the pineapple and glacé cherries in the
syrup glazed dish. Carefully spread sponge mixture
over the fruit. Bake at 350°F/180°C/Gas Mark 4 for
45–55 minutes. To serve turn the pudding out onto a
warmed plate.
Serves 4.

BAKED ALASKA

1 quantity victoria
sandwich mixture (see
page 87)
2–4 tbsp./40–80ml rum or
sherry (optional)
3 egg whites
4oz./100g caster sugar

17fl.oz./480ml block
vanilla ice cream
12oz./300g frozen fruit,
thawed, e.g.
blackcurrants,
blackberries, raspberries

Grease an 8 inch/20cm flan tin. Prepare victoria
sandwich mixture and turn into flan tin. Bake at
375°F/190°C/Gas Mark 5 for 20–25 minutes. Turn
out and allow to cool on wire tray.

Sprinkle sponge with rum or sherry. Whisk the egg
whites until they are stiff and form peaks. Whisk in
half the sugar and fold in the remainder with a metal
spoon.

Place the block of ice cream onto flan base cutting
to fit if necessary. Arrange the fruit on the top and
around the edge to make a dome shape. Cover the
whole flan base with the meringue. Bake for about
5 minutes at 450°F/230°C/Gas Mark 8 until golden.
Serve immediately.
Serves 5.

BUTTERFLY CAKES

1 quantity victoria
sandwich mixture (see
page 87)

Butter Icing
4oz./100g butter, softened
8oz./200g icing sugar
few drops vanilla essence

Divide the sandwich mixture between 18 well-buttered bun tins or paper cases. Bake at 375°F/190°C/Gas Mark 5 for 15–20 minutes or until well risen and golden. Cool on a wire rack.

Prepare the butter icing by beating the butter and icing sugar together with the essence until a very smooth, soft mixture is obtained.

To make the butterflies, cut a slice from the top of each cake, and spoon on a little butter icing. Cut the cake slices in half and put into cream at an angle to form wings. Dust lightly with icing sugar.
Makes approximately 18 cakes.

JAM SPONGE PUDDING

4oz./100g butter or
margarine
4oz./100g caster sugar
2 eggs

6oz./150g self-raising flour
2 tbsp./40ml milk
2 tbsp./40ml jam
caster sugar to dredge

Prepare the victoria sponge mixture (see page 87). As this recipe requires an extra 2oz./50g flour, use enough milk to give a soft dropping consistency. The mixture should drop from the spoon without shaking.

Grease the pudding basin and place the jam in the bottom. Pour the sponge mixture on top. Cover the top of basin with a doubled piece of greaseproof paper, making a pleat across the centre. The pleat allows the pudding to rise during cooking. Secure the paper round the pudding basin with string. Steam for approximately 1½ hours, refilling the steamer with boiling water when necessary.

The following variations can be made to the flavouring:

Syrup
Place 2 tbsp./40ml golden syrup in the bottom of basin.

Apple
Stew and sweeten 8oz./200g cooking apples. Put in bottom of pudding basin and cover with sponge.

LEMON SPONGE PUDDING

2oz./50g margarine
4oz./100g caster sugar
finely grated rind and juice
of 2 lemons

2 eggs, separated
½ pint/250ml milk
2oz./50g self-raising flour

Cream margarine and sugar together with the lemon rind until pale and fluffy. Add the egg yolks and beat in well. Stir in half the milk, then the flour. Pour in the rest of the milk and lemon juice. Whisk the egg whites in a clean bowl, until they hold their shape and fold them into the mixture with a metal spoon. Pour into a greased 2 pint/1 litre oven dish and place in a roasting tin half filled with water. Cook in the centre of a moderate oven 325°F/170°C/Gas Mark 3 for about 1 hour. This pudding will separate into a sponge on the top and sauce at the base.
Serves 4–5.

LEMON CAKE

4oz./100g butter or
   margarine
5oz./125g caster sugar
2 eggs
2 tbsp./40ml milk
6oz./150g self-raising flour
grated rind of 1 lemon

Topping
juice of 1 lemon
3 tbsp./60ml icing sugar

Butter Icing
4oz./100g icing sugar
2oz./50g butter
grated rind of 1 lemon
few drops lemon juice

Grease and line two 6 inch/15cm sandwich tins. Cream the butter, caster sugar and lemon rind until light and fluffy. Add the eggs, one at a time, beating well. Fold in the flour with a metal spoon and add sufficient milk to give a soft dropping consistency.

The mixture should drop from the spoon without shaking.

Divide the mixture into the sandwich tins. Bake at 350°F/180°C/Gas Mark 4 for approximately 30 minutes or until cooked. While the cakes are cooking prepare the topping by mixing the lemon juice with the icing sugar. Remove the cakes from tins onto a wire rack. Whilst hot, spoon the topping onto one sandwich. Allow to cool.

Make the butter icing by creaming butter, lemon rind and icing sugar together, adding a few drops of lemon juice to make a soft consistency. Ensuring that the half containing the topping is on the top sandwich the two halves of the cake together with the butter icing.

MARBLE CAKE

6oz./150g margarine
6oz./150g caster sugar
3 eggs
6oz./150g self-raising flour
6 tsp./30ml cocoa powder
6 tsp./30ml instant coffee
   powder, dissolved in a
   little warm water

Icing
3 tbsp./60ml apricot jam
2oz./50g coconut,
   dessicated
4oz./100g icing sugar
few drops lemon juice
water to mix
½–1 tsp./2.5–5ml cocoa
   powder, dissolved in a
   little warm water

Cream the margarine and sugar together until light and fluffy. Beat in the eggs one at a time and fold in the flour. Divide the mixture into three equal portions. To one portion add the cocoa powder, and to another add the coffee mixture.

Grease and line a 7 inch/18cm round cake tin. Place fairly large spoonfuls of the three mixtures randomly into the tin and smooth the top. With a skewer swirl a circle from the outside into middle. Bake at 375°F/190°C/Gas Mark 5 for 45–60 minutes until cooked. Remove from tin and cool on a wire rack.

When cold, trim the top of the cake to flatten. Cover the sides with warmed jam, and roll in the toasted coconut. Sieve the icing sugar, add a few drops of lemon juice and sufficient water to make a fairly thick icing. Reserve approximately 1 tbsp./20ml of the icing and mix it with the cocoa dissolved in water to give a chocolate icing.

Spread the white icing over the top of the cake right to the edges, then pipe lines of chocolate icing across the cake. With a skewer draw the icing one way and then back the other to form a feather icing pattern.

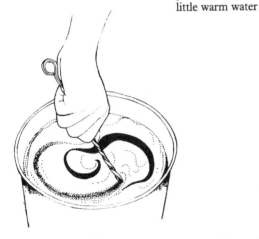

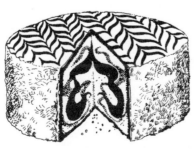

ORANGE CHIP CAKE

4oz./100g margarine
4oz./100g caster sugar
grated rind of ½ orange
4oz./100g self-raising flour
2 eggs
1 tbsp./20ml orange juice
2oz./50g chocolate, grated
2oz./50g walnuts, finely
   chopped

Filling
2oz./50g butter
4oz./100g icing sugar
rind of 1 orange
2 tsp./10ml orange juice

Grease and line two 6½ inch/16.5cm sandwich tins. Cream margarine, sugar and orange rind together until pale and fluffy. Add eggs one at a time beating to a smooth consistency. Fold in the sieved flour, chopped nuts, grated chocolate and orange juice and mix until all ingredients are incorporated. Bake at 375°F/190°C/Gas Mark 5 for 25 minutes. Remove from tins and cool on a wire rack.

Combine the filling ingredients together and beat until the mixture is smooth and soft. Sandwich the two cakes together.

CHOCOLATE CAKE

8oz./200g margarine
10oz./250g caster sugar
4 eggs
10oz./250g self-raising
   flour
2oz./50g cocoa
4 tbsp./80ml milk

Icing
10oz./250g unsalted butter
   or margarine
1¼lb./500g icing sugar
1 tbsp./20ml cocoa
few drops vanilla essence
3–4oz./75–100g flaked
   almonds, toasted
6 small or 3 large chocolate
   flakes

Cream margarine and sugar together until light and fluffy. Add the eggs one at a time beating well. Sieve the cocoa and flour together and fold into the cake mixture, adding sufficient milk to make a soft dropping consistency.

Turn into a greased 8inch/20cm round cake tin and bake at 350°F/180°C/Gas Mark 4 for approximately 1 hour 20 minutes until cooked. Remove from tin and allow to cool on a wire rack. When cold split cake into three layers.

Cream the butter and icing sugar together until light and fluffy. Divide in half. To one half add the cocoa powder, to the other a few drops of vanilla essence.

Sandwich the three layers of the cake together with some of the chocolate flavoured butter icing. Coat the sides of the cake with some of the vanilla butter icing. Spread the almonds on a large sheet of greaseproof paper. Turn the cake on its side and, holding lightly, carefully roll it across the almonds to coat the sides. Cover the top of the cake with the vanilla butter icing and then arrange the chocolate flakes in triangles across the top, cutting large ones in half and trimming the smaller ones if necessary. With a forcing bag, pipe a triangle of alternate chocolate and vanilla icing between the chocolate flakes, and finally pipe a chocolate rosette in the middle.

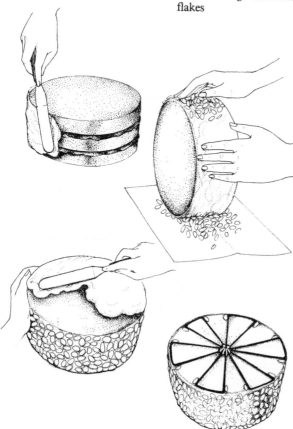

BREAKFAST BUNS

2oz./50g butter
1oz./25g lard
4oz./100g caster sugar
1 egg
8oz./200g ordinary plain
   flour
1½ tsp./7.5ml baking
   powder
pinch ground nutmeg
½ tsp./2.5ml salt
4fl.oz./100ml milk

To finish
2oz./50g caster sugar
1½oz./40g melted butter
1 tsp./5ml ground
   cinnamon

Grease 12 patty tins. Beat the butter, lard, sugar and egg together. Sieve the flour, baking powder, nutmeg and salt together and beat into the egg mixture with the milk.

Spoon the mixture into the greased patty tins, bake at 350°F/180°C/Gas Mark 4 for approximately 25 minutes. Remove from tin.

Prick the buns on the top and brush with the melted butter, sprinkle on the remaining caster sugar and cinnamon. Serve hot.

Makes approximately 12 buns.

APPLE AND NUT CAKE

8oz./200g caster sugar
4oz./100g margarine
2 eggs, beaten
2oz./50g nuts, chopped
5oz./125g raisins, chopped
8oz./200g ordinary plain
   flour or wholemeal flour

½ tsp./2.5ml bicarbonate
   of soda
pinch nutmeg
1 tsp./5ml mixed spice
8oz./200g unsweetened
   stewed apple

Beat the sugar and margarine together until light and fluffy. Beat the eggs in well. Stir in the nuts and raisins. Sift together the flour, bicarbonate of soda, nutmeg and mixed spice. Add alternately with the stewed apple to the mixture, beating well after each addition. When mixed turn into a greased and lined 7 inch/18cm square cake tin. Bake at 350°F/180°C/Gas Mark 4 for approximately 1¼ hours. Remove from tin and cool on a wire rack.

MADELEINES

4oz./100g butter or
   margarine
4oz./100g caster sugar
2 eggs
4oz./100g self-raising flour
2 tbsp./40ml red jam,
   melted

Decoration
desiccated coconut
glacé cherries and angelica

Grease 10–12 dariole moulds. Cream the fat and sugar until pale and fluffy. Add the eggs one at a time, beating well after each addition. Fold in the flour with a metal spoon. Three-quarters fill the moulds and bake in the oven at 350°F/180°C/Gas Mark 4 for about 20 minutes, or until firm and browned. Turn cakes out of the moulds and leave to cool on wire rack. Trim the bottoms, so that the cakes stand firmly and are of even height. When they are nearly cold, brush with melted jam. Securing each madeleine with a skewer through the base roll them in coconut. Top each madeleine with a glacé cherry and two small angelica 'leaves'.

Note: For the traditional French madeleines, Genoese mixture is baked in special well-greased fluted shell-shape tins.

Makes approximately 12 madeleines.

MADEIRA CAKE

6oz./150g butter, softened
6oz./150g caster sugar
grated rind of ½ lemon
3 eggs

8oz./200g self-raising flour
½ tsp./2.5ml salt
1 tbsp./20ml water
piece of candied lemon peel

Warm the mixing bowl whilst weighing out the ingredients. Place the butter, sugar and grated lemon rind in the bowl. Beat together until light and fluffy.

Add the eggs one at a time, beating to a smooth consistency between each addition. Add a spoonful of flour with the last egg. Fold the remainder of the flour with the salt and the water into the mixture.

Cook in a greased lined 7 inch/18cm round tin for approximately 1½ hours at 350°F/180°C/Gas Mark 4. After the first 25 minutes carefully place a piece of candied lemon peel on top of the cake. When cooked remove from tin, and cool on a wire rack.

Coconut Cake

Make up the Madeira Cake recipe (see above) adding ½ tsp./2.5ml vanilla essence instead of lemon rind. Replace 2oz./50g flour with the same amount of dessicated coconut.

LAYER CAKE

5 eggs, separated
6oz./150g caster sugar
5oz./125g ordinary plain flour
pinch salt
2 tsp./10ml baking powder
few drops vanilla essence

Icing
2 eggs
6oz./150g butter
8oz./200g icing sugar
4oz./100g plain chocolate, grated
maraschino cherries
few drops vanilla essence

Warm bowl and whisk. Whisk egg yolks and sugar until thick and creamy. Fold in the flour, salt, baking powder and vanilla essence. Whisk whites until stiff and fold into the batter. Pour into a greased 8 inch/20cm round cake tin. Bake at 350°F/180°C/Gas Mark 4 for approximately 45 minutes.

Icing
Whisk the eggs with half the sugar until thick and creamy. Cream the butter, the remaining sugar and vanilla essence until light and creamy. Combine the two mixtures together with the whisk.

Cut the cake into three layers, and spread each layer with some of the cream. Sprinkle the chocolate onto the cream, put the cake back together and decorate with maraschino cherries.

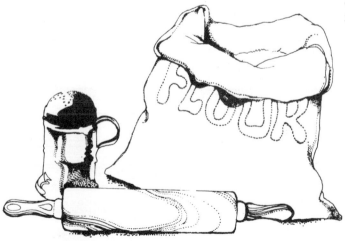

RASPBERRY SWISS ROLL

Sponge
2 eggs
2oz./50g caster sugar
2oz./50g ordinary plain
   flour

Filling
½ pint/250ml double
   cream
1 tbsp./20ml caster sugar
8oz./200g frozen or fresh
   raspberries, drained

Put the eggs and sugar in a large bowl over a pan of hot water and whisk until thick, light and creamy, and leaves a trail behind. Sift the flour and fold lightly into the mixture with a metal spoon. Pour the mixture into a greased and lined Swiss Roll tin 7¾ × 11¾ inches/18 × 28cm. Bake at 425°F/220°C/Gas Mark 7 for 7–9 minutes until brown and springs back when lightly touched. Turn onto a piece of greaseproof paper sprinkled with caster sugar. Trim the edges and make a cut ½ inch/12mm from the short edge and roll up. Place onto a wire rack and allow to cool.

Reserve a few raspberries for decoration. Whip cream until stiff, keeping back approximately one third for decoration. Fold the sugar and fruit into the remaining cream.

Unroll and spread the filling over the Swiss Roll. Roll up, pipe on the remaining cream and decorate with raspberries.
Serves 4–5.

STRAWBERRY APRICOT GÂTEAU

Sponge
3 eggs
3oz./75g caster sugar
3oz./75g self-raising flour

Filling
¼ pint/125ml double
   cream
sugar to taste
8oz./200g strawberries
8oz./200g apricots

Clean and halve the strawberries. Halve the apricots and remove the stones and cook gently in a very little water with sugar to taste until soft. Drain and cool.

Whisk the eggs and sugar in a warmed bowl or in a bowl over a pan of hot water until thick enough to leave a trail.

Carefully fold the flour with a metal spoon into the whisked mixture. Pour into two 7 inch/18cm greased and lined sandwich tins. Cook for approximately 20 minutes at 350°F/180°C/Gas Mark 4. Remove from tins. Cool on a wire rack.

Whisk the cream until stiff, adding sugar to taste. Chop the apricots and a third of the strawberries and mix with half the cream. Sandwich the two cakes together with this mixture. Spread the remaining cream on the top of the cake and decorate the top with the remaining strawberry halves.
Serves 4–5.

COFFEE AND HAZELNUT GÂTEAU

4 eggs, separated
4oz./100g caster sugar
2 tbsp./40ml coffee essence
4oz./100g ordinary plain
 flour

Butter Cream
6oz./150g butter
10oz./250g icing sugar
2 tbsp./40ml coffee essence

Glacé Icing
4oz./100g icing sugar
1 tbsp./20ml coffee essence
1 tbsp./20ml warm water
 (approximately)

To decorate
4oz./100g hazelnuts,
 toasted and finely
 chopped
 (approximately)

Warm bowl and whisk. Whisk egg yolks and sugar until mixture is thick, pale and leaves a trail. Whisk in coffee essence then fold flour gently into mixture. Whisk the egg whites until stiff and form peaks. Fold into the batter with a metal spoon.

Spoon the sponge into a loose bottomed 8inch/20cm round cake tin. Bake at 350°F/180°C/Gas Mark 4 for about 40–50 minutes until well risen and firm to touch. Leave in the tin for 5 minutes before turning out. When cool split cake into three horizontal slices.

Cream together all the butter cream ingredients. Using half the butter cream, sandwich the layers together. Reserving a small amount for decoration, spread the remaining butter cream round the sides of the cake. Sprinkle the chopped hazelnuts on a piece of greaseproof paper. Roll the cake in the chopped hazelnuts so they are evenly distributed round the sides. Make the glacé icing by mixing the coffee essence and warm water with the sieved icing sugar. The icing should coat the back of a wooden spoon. Pour the icing on top of the cake. Decorate with rosettes of butter cream.

GENOESE SPONGE

Genoese sponges are generally used as a base for gateaux or for rich or highly decorated cakes.

2½oz./65g butter
3 eggs
3oz./75g caster sugar
3oz./75g plain flour, sifted
 twice

Brush two 7 inch/18cm sandwich tins with ½oz./15g melted butter. Line the base with rounds of greaseproof. Dust lightly with flour.

Melt the remaining butter over a low heat, strain into a clean basin through muslin. Whisk eggs in a basin over a saucepan of hand hot water for 2 minutes. Add sugar, continue whisking until the mixture is thick and leaves a trail. Remove from heat and continue whisking until the mixture is cool. If using a mixer warm the bowl and beaters before whisking the eggs and sugar. There is no need to whisk over hot water with an electric mixer. With a large metal spoon, gently fold in half of the melted butter and half of the flour. Repeat with remaining butter and flour.

Transfer to tins and bake at 350°F/180°C/Gas Mark 4 for 25 minutes or until golden and shrunk slightly away from the sides.

Leave in tins for 1 minute. Turn onto a folded tea-towel, remove paper. Cool.

Sandwich together as desired. This cake keeps well in an airtight tin.

WHOLEMEAL FRUIT CAKE

6oz./150g margarine
6oz./150g caster sugar
3 eggs
12oz./300g wholemeal
   flour
1½ tsp./7.5ml baking
   powder
1 level tsp./5ml grated
   nutmeg

1 tsp./5ml cinnamon
12oz./300g mixed dried
   fruit
2oz./50g mixed peel
2oz./50g glacé cherries,
   halved
grated rind of 1 lemon
1–2 tbsp./20–40ml milk

Grease and line an 8 inch/20cm cake tin. Warm the mixing bowl whilst weighing out the ingredients. Beat the margarine and sugar together until light and fluffy. Beat in the eggs one at a time, adding a spoonful of flour with the last egg. Sift flour, baking powder and spice together. Add the flour, fruit and spices and enough milk to give a smooth consistency. Pour into a prepared cake tin and bake at 325°F/170°C/Gas Mark 3 for 2–2½ hours or until cooked. A skewer will come out clean from the cake when it is cooked. Remove from tin and cool on a wire rack.

DUNDEE CAKE

6oz./150g margarine
6oz./150g brown sugar
grated rind ½ lemon
3 eggs
10oz./250g ordinary plain
   flour
½ tsp./2.5ml salt
8oz./200g sultanas
6oz./150g currants
2oz./50g mixed peel
2oz./50g glacé cherries,
   halved
2oz./50g ground or
   chopped almonds
1 tbsp./20ml milk

To decorate
1oz./25g blanched split
   almonds

Cream fat, sugar and lemon rind until light and fluffy. Add eggs one at a time, adding 1 tbsp./20ml flour with the last egg. Fold in the remaining flour, salt, fruit, nuts and milk to give a soft consistency. Transfer to a greased and lined 7 inch/18cm round cake tin, and arrange the split almonds on top. Bake 300°F/150°C/Gas Mark 2 for 2½–3 hours approximately. Allow to cool in the tin.

STOUT CAKE

8oz./200g margarine
8oz./200g brown sugar
2 eggs
3oz./75g almonds,
   blanched and roughly
   chopped
4oz./100g currants
6oz./150g sultanas

12oz./300g ordinary plain
   flour
3 tsp./15ml baking powder
1 tsp./5ml mixed spice
¼ pint/125ml plus 2
   tbsp./40ml stout

Cream margarine and sugar together until light and fluffy. Beat eggs and add gradually to the creamed mixture. Add the almonds, currants and sultanas. Sift the flour, baking powder and mixed spice together and fold into the creamed mixture alternately with approximately ¼ pint/125ml stout, adding a little more if necessary to give a soft consistency.

Grease and line an 8 inch/20cm round cake tin. Pour in the mixture and bake in the centre of the oven at 300°F/150°C/Gas Mark 2 for approximately 2¼–2½ hours. Test the cake with a skewer; if it comes out clean the cake is cooked. Cool in the tin.

When cold prick the cake all over with a skewer and spoon 1 tbsp./20ml stout over the top. Treat the base in the same manner. Wrap in foil and keep for two days before eating.

CHRISTMAS CAKE

This cake should be made at least two months before Christmas to allow the flavour to develop. It is kept moist in foil with the addition of a little brandy during Advent.

12oz./300g unsalted butter, softened

10oz./250g soft brown sugar

8 eggs

12oz./300g self-raising flour

3 tsp./15ml mixed spice

½ tsp./2.5ml salt

1 tsp./5ml ground nutmeg

1 tsp./5ml ground cloves

1lb./400g stoned raisins, chopped

1lb/400g currants

1lb/400g sultanas

8oz./200g glacé cherries, quartered

8oz./200g mixed peel, chopped (the kind of peel that you chop yourself is nicest)

1oz./25g angelica, finely chopped

4oz./100g almonds, blanched and chopped

4oz./100g ground almonds

4 tbsp./80ml brandy

grated rind and juice of 1 lemon

Butter a round 10inch/24cm cake tin. Line with two or three thicknesses of greaseproof paper (brushed with melted butter) to stand well above the tin. Around the outside tie four thicknesses of brown paper.

Beat the softened butter with the sugar until pale and fluffy. Beat in the eggs one by one. Combine with the dry ingredients, fruit, and lastly the brandy and lemon juice. If the mixture is not soft and moist beat in another egg and a dash of milk. Transfer to the prepared tin making a slight well in the centre of the mixture. Bake below the centre of the oven at 300°F/150°C/Gas Mark 2 for 1½ hours; then at 250°F/130°C/Gas Mark ½ for 3½ hours. Take great care not to overbake or the cake will dry out. Test the cake with a skewer. If it comes out clean the cake is cooked. During the last few hours, cover the cake with several thicknesses of brown paper to prevent overbrowning and sit the tin on several thicknesses of newspaper. Cool cake in the tin. Remove from tin when cold, and wrap in foil.

Two months before Christmas unwrap and pierce the base several times with a skewer. Pour over approximately 5 tbsp./100ml brandy. Repack. Repeat two weeks before Christmas. Spread the cake with apricot jam and cover with almond paste (see page 99). Allow to dry and then cover with Royal Icing (see page 99). Allow to dry and decorate.

A Guide for Almond Pasting and Icing Rich Cakes

Ingredients	Round Square	7 inches/18 cm 6 inches/15cm	8 inches/20cm 7 inches/18cm	9 inches/22.5cm 8 inches/20cm	10 inches/25cm 9 inches/22.5cm
			Size of Tins		
Almond Paste					
Ground Almonds		6oz./150g	8oz./200g	12oz./300g	1lb./400g
Caster Sugar		4oz./100g	6oz./150g	8oz./200g	12oz./300g
Icing Sugar		4oz./100g	6oz./150g	8oz./200g	12oz./300g
Eggs		½–1	1	1–1½	2
Almond Essence		¼ tsp./1.5ml	½ tsp./2.5ml	1 tsp./5ml	1½ tsp./7.5ml
Lemon Juice		½ tsp./2.5ml	1 tsp./5ml	2 tsp./10ml	3 tsp./15ml
Orange Flower Water		¼ tsp./1.5ml	½ tsp./2.5ml	1¼ tsp./6.5ml	2 tsp./10ml
Royal Icing (coating)					
Egg Whites (large)		2	3	3	4
Icing Sugar (approximately)		1lb./400g	1lb. 5oz./525g	1lb. 5oz./525g	1lb. 12oz./700g
Glycerine		½ tsp./2.5ml	½ tsp./2.5ml	1 tsp./5ml	1½ tsp./7.5ml
Royal Icing (piping)					
Egg Whites		1	1	2	2
Icing Sugar (approximately)		7oz./175g	7oz./175g	14oz./350g	14oz./350g
Glycerine		¼ tsp./1.5ml	¼ tsp./1.5ml	½ tsp./2.5ml	½ tsp./2.5ml

Almond Paste

Mix ground almonds and icing and caster sugar together in bowl. Blend in eggs and almond essence, lemon juice and orange flower water to make a soft paste. Knead until a smooth dough is formed. Divide paste into three. Use one-third for top and remainder for sides of cake. Brush sides of cake with apricot jam before covering with almond paste. Allow paste to dry for three days before covering with royal icing.

Royal Icing

Whisk egg whites until frothy. Add icing sugar, a tablespoonful at a time, beating well after each addition. Finally, beat in the glycerine. Lemon juice makes a softer icing and may also be added at this stage. Cover bowl with damp cloth to prevent icing hardening.

GINGERBREAD

Gingerbread can be made with either half wholemeal or all wholemeal flour by substituting the following ingredients in the basic gingerbread recipe.

4oz./100g margarine
6oz./150g black treacle
2oz./50g golden syrup
¼ pint/125ml milk
2oz./50g sugar
8oz./200g ordinary plain flour
1 tbsp./20ml ground ginger
1 tsp./5ml bicarbonate of soda
2 eggs, well beaten
1oz./25g chopped nuts, e.g. hazelnuts or almonds
1oz./25g sultanas
1oz./25g chopped peel

Half wholemeal
4oz./100g ordinary plain flour
5oz./125g wholemeal flour

All wholemeal
4oz./100g black treacle
4oz./100g golden syrup
10oz./250g wholemeal flour

Melt the margarine, treacle, sugar and syrup together gently in a large pan. Stir until the sugar dissolves. Remove from heat, add milk and allow to cool. Sieve the dry ingredients into a bowl. Add the syrup to the eggs. Stir the syrup mixture into the dry ingredients and fruit with a wooden spoon until a smooth batter is formed. Pour into a greased and lined tin 7 inches/18cm square × 1inch/2.5cm deep or 1lb./400g loaf tin. Cook for 1–1½ hours at 350°F/150°C/Gas Mark 2. When cooked remove from tin and cool on a wire rack.

AMERICAN DATE AND WALNUT MUFFINS

4oz./100g ordinary plain flour
pinch salt
1½ tsp./7.5ml baking powder
1oz./25g caster sugar

1 large egg
1oz./25g butter, melted
4fl.oz./100ml milk
1oz./25g chopped dates
1oz./25g chopped walnuts

Grease nine patty tins. Sift the flour, salt and baking powder into a bowl, add the sugar, dates and walnuts. Beat the egg with the butter and milk and add to the dry ingredients. Mix quickly and divide between the patty tins.

Bake at 400°F/200°C/Gas Mark 6 for 20–25 minutes. Remove from tins. Cool on a wire rack.
Makes approximately 9 muffins.

SUMMER PUDDING

1lb./400g mixture of soft fruit, e.g. redcurrants, blackcurrants, raspberries, etc.

¼ pint/125ml water
3 tbsp./60ml granulated sugar
6–7 slices white bread

Wash the fruit and put into a pan with the water and sugar. Bring to the boil and simmer gently until soft, leave to cool, and sweeten to taste.

Line a 1 pint/500ml pudding basin with the bread slices with the crusts removed. Make sure that any gaps are filled with wedges of bread. Pour half the fruit mixture into the lined basin. Add a slice of bread with the crusts removed. Pour the remainder of the fruit mixture. Add the remaining bread to make a carefully fitting lid. Put a plate on top with a weight on it and leave overnight.

Turn out carefully and serve with thick double cream.

REFRIGERATOR CAKE

16oz./400g digestive biscuits, crushed
3oz./75g chopped nuts, e.g. hazelnuts or almonds
3–4oz./75–100g plain chocolate, melted in a basin over hot water

Sauce
3oz./75g soya flour
1½oz./40g cocoa powder
3oz./75g butter
2oz./50g caster sugar
½ pint/250ml milk
3oz./75g marshmallows, quartered

Break the biscuits and place in a polythene bag. Securing the open end press a rolling pin over the biscuits until they are completely crushed.

Place all the sauce ingredients into a double saucepan and heat gently, stirring continuously. Heat to nearly boiling point and cook for approximately 5 minutes until the mixture thickens and becomes glossy in appearance. Allow the sauce to cool. Mix in the biscuits and nuts and turn into lightly greased tin 11½ × 7½ × 1 inch/29 × 19 × 2.5cm approximately and chill in the refrigerator. Cover with the melted chocolate and allow to set. When thoroughly chilled cut into squares.

WHOLEMEAL BANANA LOAF

This recipe calls for all wholemeal flour, but if you prefer you may substitute 4oz./100g plain white flour for 4oz./100g wholemeal flour.

If milling your own flour select a soft wheat.

8oz./200g wholemeal flour
1 level tsp./5ml baking powder
pinch salt
3oz./75g margarine
2oz./50g caster sugar

1 tbsp./20ml golden syrup
1 banana, peeled
1 egg, beaten
2 tbsp./40ml lemon juice

Mix the flour thoroughly with the salt and baking powder. Melt the margarine, sugar and syrup gently in a pan. Purée the banana by mashing or dropping onto liquidiser blades through the feed hole in the lid. Combine the banana thoroughly with the flour, eggs and melted mixture. Pour into a greased and lined 2lb./800g loaf tin. Bake in the centre of the oven 350°/180°C/Gas Mark 4 for 50–55 minutes or until cooked. Turn out of the tin and cool on a wire rack. This loaf is good served cold, sliced and spread with butter.

DEVIL'S FOOD CAKE

1 quantity chocolate
victoria sandwich
mixture
(see page 87)

Frosting
1lb./400g granulated sugar
¼ pint/125ml cold water
2 egg whites

chocolate flake to decorate

Divide chocolate sandwich mixture between two well-greased 7 inch/18cm sandwich tins. Bake at 350°F/180°C/Gas Mark 4 for 25–30 minutes. Turn out of tins and cool on a wire tray.

Prepare the frosting by heating sugar and water in a heavy-based saucepan. Bring to the boil. Allow mixture to boil, without stirring, until a teaspoonful forms a soft ball when dropped into cold water. Pour cooled syrup onto lightly beaten egg whites and whisk until the mixture is thick and coats the back of a wooden spoon.

Use a third of the frosting straight away to sandwich cakes together, and spread the remainder over the sides and top. Decorate with chocolate flakes.

ORANGE CAKE

4oz./100g butter
4oz./100g caster sugar
2 eggs, separated
grated rind and juice of
1 large orange
4oz./100g self-raising flour

To decorate
blanched orange peel
glacé icing

Grease a 6 inch/15cm round cake tin. Cream the butter and caster sugar until light and fluffy. Add the egg yolks one at a time and mix in well. Blend in the orange rind and juice with 1 tablespoon of flour and fold in the remaining flour. Whisk the egg whites until stiff and form peaks and gently fold into the flour mixture. Turn immediately into the prepared cake tin and bake at 375°F/190°C/Gas Mark 5 for 25 minutes or until the cake is golden brown and springs back when lightly pressed. Turn out of tin and cool on a wire rack. To decorate the cake pare thin strips of orange peel and blanch by dropping in boiling water for 1 minute. Pat dry with kitchen paper. When the cake is completely cold cover the top with glacé icing (see page 96) and sprinkle the orange slivers on top.

HONEY LOAF

6oz./150g clear honey
¼ pint/125ml milk
12oz./300g self-raising
flour
1 tsp./5ml salt
4oz./100g soft brown sugar
3 tsp./15ml mixed spice
1oz./25g sultanas
1oz./25g walnuts, chopped

Topping
2oz./50g lump sugar

Grease two 1lb./400g loaf tins. Heat honey and milk together and allow to cool. Sift dry ingredients together and mix in sugar, sultanas and nuts. Add milk and honey liquid and mix to form a smooth, stiff mixture. Turn into tins, crumble lump sugar on top and bake at 350°F/180°C/Gas Mark 4 for 1¼ hours. Remove from tins and cool loaves on wire rack. Serve sliced with butter.

SEED CAKE

6oz./150g butter
6oz./150g caster sugar
3 eggs
1 tsp./5ml orange flower
water (optional)
12oz./300g ordinary plain
flour

1½ tsp./7.5ml baking
powder
¼ tsp./1.5ml salt
2 tbsp./40ml caraway
seeds
grated rind 1 orange

Cream butter and sugar until light and fluffy and beat in the eggs one at a time. Add the orange flower water, fold in the flour, baking powder and salt and add caraway seeds and orange rind. Mix until all ingredients are incorporated. Grease and line the base of an 8 inch/20cm round cake tin. Pour the mixture into tin and bake at 350°F/180°C/Gas Mark 4 for 45–50 minutes. Allow cake to cool in tin for five minutes and then turn out on to wire rack.

APRICOT NUT SLICES

4oz./100g dried apricots
4oz./100g margarine
4oz./100g caster sugar
6oz./150g self-raising flour
8oz./200g soft brown sugar
2 eggs, beaten

large pinch of salt
1½ tsp./7.5ml vanilla
essence
2oz./50g walnuts, chopped

Rinse apricots, cover with water, bring to boil and simmer for 10 minutes. Drain, cool and chop. Cream fat with caster sugar and stir in 4oz./100g of flour. Turn mixture into a greased 8 inch/20cm square cake tin and bake at 350°F/180°C/Gas Mark 4 for 20 minutes. Remove tin and keep oven at same temperature.

Mix brown sugar into eggs beating well after each addition. Stir in remaining sifted flour and salt. Stir in apricots, vanilla essence and walnuts. Spread mixture over baked layer and return to oven and bake for 25 minutes. Cool in tin and cut into slices.

BRANDY SNAPS

2oz./50g butter
3 tbsp./60g golden syrup
2oz./50g plain flour
pinch of salt
1 tsp./5ml ground ginger
2oz./50g caster sugar
1 tsp./5ml brandy
   (optional)
1 tsp./5ml lemon juice

Filling
5fl.oz./150ml double
   cream, whipped

Melt the butter, golden syrup, sugar and lemon juice over a gentle heat, stirring all the time. Remove from heat. Sieve the dry ingredients together and stir into the treacle mixture. Add the brandy and mix well. Drop teaspoonfuls of mixture onto greased baking trays. As brandy snaps spread during cooking, make sure that there is plenty of room between each teaspoon of mixture. Bake at 350°F/180°C/Gas Mark 4 for approximately 10 minutes.

Remove from oven and allow to cool for a moment or so. Before they begin to harden, curl the brandy snaps around the handles of greased wooden spoons. Allow to harden on the spoons, then remove. Pipe the ends with whipped cream before serving.
Makes approximately 30 brandy snaps.

FLAPJACKS

3oz./75g margarine
3oz./75g caster sugar

2 tbsp./40ml golden syrup
10oz./250g wholemeal
   flour

Melt the margarine, sugar and syrup together in a pan. Add flour and stir until incorporated thoroughly. Press into a greased shallow tin about 8 inches/20cm square, and smooth the top. Bake at 325°F/170°C/Gas Mark 3 for 20–25 minutes. Remove from oven. Score surface into fingers, allow to cool in tin before removing.
Makes approximately 16 flapjacks.

DIGESTIVE BISCUITS

4oz./100g ordinary plain
   flour
8oz./200g wholemeal flour

½ tsp./2.5mg salt
3oz./75g margarine
2oz./50g lard
2oz./50g caster sugar
cold water
1 egg

Place flour in bowl, add salt and rub in fat until the mixture resembles breadcrumbs. Mix in the sugar, beat in the egg and add about 4 tbsp./80ml of cold water, and mix to a firm dough. Knead lightly. Roll out on a lightly floured surface to a thickness of ⅛inch/3mm. Prick with a fork and cut into 2½ inch/6cm rounds with a plain cutter. Knead trimmings together, re-roll and repeat. Place onto two greased baking trays and bake at 350°F/180°C/Gas Mark 4 for approximately 24 minutes. Cool on wire rack.
Makes approximately 40 biscuits.

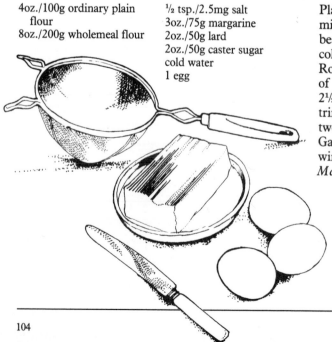

FINNISH STICKS

8oz./200g butter
3oz./75g caster sugar
1 tsp./5ml almond essence
10oz./250g ordinary plain
  flour

Finish
little beaten egg
2oz./50g nibbed almonds
2 tsp./10ml caster sugar

Cream butter and sugar together. Add almond essence and flour to form a smooth dough. Roll out the dough between ¼–½ inch/6–12mm thick on a lightly floured surface. Cut into fingers 3 × ½ inches/7 × 1.2cm and place onto a greased baking sheet. Brush with beaten egg, sprinkle with sugar and almonds. Bake at 350°F/180°C/Gas Mark 4 for approximately 20 minutes. Cool on a wire rack.
Makes approximately 50 biscuits.

VIENNESE TARTLETS

8oz./200g butter
2oz./50g icing sugar
8oz./200g ordinary plain
  flour
few drops vanilla essence

To decorate
red jam
icing sugar

Cream butter with icing sugar until soft. Gradually work in the flour and add vanilla essence. Put mixture into a piping bag fitted with a large star pipe. Pipe into paper cases, starting at the base and working up the sides with a spiral movement. Leave a slight hollow in the middle. Bake at 350°F/180°C/Gas Mark 4 for 20–25 minutes. Cool on a wire rack. When cold, sift over some icing sugar and place a little red jam in the centre.
Makes approximately 18 tartlets.

BOURBON BISCUITS

3oz./75g ordinary plain
  flour
1 tbsp./20ml custard
  powder
1 tbsp./20mg cocoa
2½oz./65g butter or
  margarine
1oz./25g caster sugar
1 egg yolk
few drops vanilla essence

Chocolate Cream Filling
3oz./75g icing sugar
1 tbsp./20ml cocoa
1½oz./40g butter
vanilla essence

Sift dry ingredients together and rub in fat. Add the sugar and mix to form a dough with the egg yolk and vanilla essence. Roll dough out to a thickness of ⅛ inch/3mm on a lightly floured board. Trim the sides and prick with a fork. Sprinkle with caster sugar and cut into fingers 1 × 3 inches/2.5 × 7.5cm. Transfer to a greased baking sheet and bake at 350°F/180°C/Gas Mark 4 for 10–15 minutes. Cool on a wire rack. To prepare filling, beat butter together with the sieved icing sugar and cocoa until creamy. When the biscuits are cold sandwich together with the filling.
Makes 13–16 biscuits.

JAMMY FACES

4oz./100g butter or
  margarine
5oz./125g caster sugar
1 egg yolk
rind of 1 lemon
8oz./200g ordinary plain
  flour
water

Filling
jam

Cream fat and sugar together. Add egg yolk and lemon rind and beat well. Stir in flour and add sufficient water to mix to a firm dough. Roll out dough to approximately $1/8$ inch/3mm thick on a floured surface. Cut into $2\frac{1}{2}$ inch/6cm rounds. On half the biscuits make two small holes for the eyes and cut out a mouth. Transfer biscuits onto a baking sheet and bake at 350°F/180°C/Gas Mark 4 for 10–15 minutes. Cool on a wire rack. Place a small teaspoon of jam on uncut round and place face on the top. Dust with icing sugar.

Makes approximately 12 biscuits.

CRUNCHY COOKIES

4oz./100g margarine
3oz./75g caster sugar
1 egg
few drops almond essence

8oz./200g wholemeal flour
1 tsp./5ml baking powder
3–4 glacé cherries

Cream margarine and sugar together. Beat in egg and almond essence. Work in flour and baking powder, sifted together. Using a 1 tsp./5ml quantity at a time roll mixture into small balls. If the mixture is too sticky rinse hands in cold water and leave hands wet while rolling. Place cookies on a greased baking sheet, $1\frac{1}{2}$–2 inches/4–5cm apart and place a small piece of glacé cherry in the centre of each cookie. Bake at 350°F/180°C/Gas Mark 4 for 25–30 minutes or until golden brown. Carefully remove cookies from baking tray while still warm and cool on a wire tray.

Makes approximately 24 cookies.

FLORENTINES

2oz./50g butter
$2\frac{1}{2}$oz./65g caster sugar
1 tbsp./20ml golden syrup
2oz./50g candied peel,
  chopped
2oz./50g flaked almonds,
  chopped

1oz./25g glacé cherries,
  chopped
2oz./50g ordinary plain
  flour
1 tbsp./20ml cream
1 tsp./5ml lemon juice
4oz./100g plain chocolate

Melt butter, sugar and golden syrup in a pan. Chop the peel, almonds and cherries and add to the melted ingredients. Mix in well the flour, lemon juice and cream. Put small spoonfuls of mixture onto a greased baking tray. Flatten slightly keeping in well-shaped rounds. Keep well apart to allow for spreading. Bake at 350°F/180°C/Gas Mark 4 for approximately 10 minutes or until golden brown. After removing from the oven press the edges of biscuits to a neat shape with a knife. When the biscuits begin to firm remove from tray and allow to cool on a wire rack. When the biscuits are cold melt chocolate in a basin over hot water and spread over the backs of the biscuits.

Makes approximately 20 florentines.

EASTER BISCUITS

6oz./150g ordinary plain flour
½ tsp./2.5ml mixed spice
½ tsp./2.5ml cinnamon

3oz./75g margarine
3oz./75g caster sugar
2oz./50g currants
1 egg

Sift flour and spices together. Rub in fat and add sugar, currants and sufficient egg to form a stiff dough. Knead lightly and roll out to a thickness of ⅛–¼ inch/3–6mm on a floured surface. Cut into rounds using a 3 inch/7.5cm fluted cutter and bake for 15–20 minutes at 350°F/180°C/Gas Mark 4. Cool on a wire rack.

Makes approximately 14 biscuits.

SHORTBREAD

This is a wholemeal version, you may of course use all white flour or a mixture of half white and half wholemeal flour. If milling your own wholemeal flour use a soft wheat. The rice flour may be milled in the wheatmill.

6oz./150g wholemeal flour
1oz./25g rice flour
4oz./100g softened butter
2oz./50g caster sugar

Rub the butter into the flour and rice flour until the mixture resembles breadcrumbs. Thoroughly mix in the caster sugar by hand. Turn into an 8 inch/20cm tin and use a fork to press into the shape of the tin. Prick the surface of the shortbread and bake at 350°F/180°C/Gas Mark 4 in the centre of oven for 30–45 minutes. Cut into portions when first out of oven, but allow to cool before removing from tin. For best results remove from tin before completely cold, and finish cooling on a wire rack.

Makes 6 shortbreads.

CHOCOLATE VIENNESE FINGERS

8oz./200g butter
2oz./50g icing sugar
2oz./50g plain chocolate, melted
8oz./200g ordinary plain flour
2 tbsp./40ml cocoa
few drops vanilla essence

Vanilla butter icing
3oz./75g butter
6oz./150g icing sugar
few drops vanilla essence
1–2 tbsp./20–40ml milk

Beat butter and icing sugar together until light and fluffy. Stir in the cooled melted chocolate and vanilla essence. Sift flour and cocoa together and fold into mixture. Using a plain nozzle, pipe fingers approximately 3 inches/7.5cm long onto a greased baking sheet. Bake at 350°F/180°C/Gas Mark 4 for 20–25 minutes. Cool on a wire rack. Prepare butter icing by beating all the ingredients together. Sandwich the fingers together with butter icing.

Makes approximately 18 fingers.

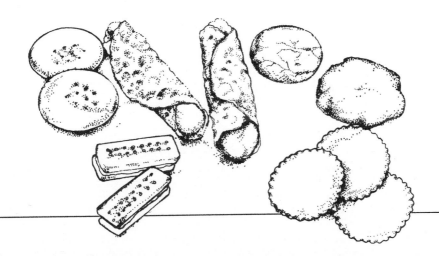

DATE AND WALNUT CRUNCHIES

6oz./150g self-raising flour
6oz./150g semolina
6oz./150g margarine
3oz./75g caster sugar

Filling
6oz./150g dates, stoned
   and chopped
1 tbsp./20ml honey
4 tbsp./80ml water
1 tbsp./20ml lemon juice
pinch mixed spice
2oz./50g walnuts, chopped

Cover the dates with boiling water and allow to stand for ½ hour. Drain. Grease a 7 inch/18cm square tin. Heat filling ingredients, except for walnuts, for approximately 5 minutes or until smooth and soft. Stir in walnuts. Mix flour and semolina. Heat margarine and sugar until fat is melted and stir into flour mixture. Place half mixture in bottom of tin and spread filling over base. Cover filling with remaining mixture, smooth the top and bake at 375°F/180°C/Gas Mark 4 for 30–35 minutes. Cut into squares and allow to cool in tin.
Makes approximately 12 squares.

LEMON ICED BISCUITS

3oz./75g butter
3oz./75g sugar
finely grated rind ½ lemon
1 egg
pinch of salt
6oz./150g ordinary plain
   flour
milk

Glacé Icing
4oz./100g icing sugar
1 tsp./5ml lemon juice
1½ tbsp./30ml warm water

Cream butter, sugar and lemon rind together until light and fluffy and beat in the egg. Mix in salt and flour to form a soft dough adding a little milk if necessary. Roll out to ⅛ inch/3mm thick. Cut into 2½ inch/6cm rounds. Place biscuits onto greased baking trays, prick with a fork and bake at 350°F/180°C/Gas Mark 4 for approximately 20 minutes or until golden brown. Cool on wire rack. To make the glacé icing, mix the sieved icing sugar with lemon juice and enough warm water until the icing coats the back of a spoon. Spread a little of the icing over each cold biscuit.
Makes approximately 30 biscuits.

CINNAMON SUGAR BISCUITS

4oz./100g plain flour
½ tsp./2.5ml ground
   nutmeg
4oz./100g soft brown sugar
2oz./50g butter
1 small egg, beaten
2 tsp./10ml milk

Topping
2oz./50g caster sugar
1 tsp./5ml ground
   cinnamon

Mix flour, nutmeg and sugar together and rub in butter until the mixture resembles breadcrumbs. Mix in the beaten egg and milk to form a firm dough. Shape dough into small balls and place on greased baking trays. Flatten the dough balls slightly. Mix the sugar and cinnamon together and sprinkle over the biscuits. Bake at 400°F/200°C/Gas Mark 6 for 10 minutes.
Makes approximately 36 biscuits.

CHOCOLATE COOKIES

1oz./25g plain chocolate
1oz./25g almonds
2oz./50g brown sugar
2oz./50g granulated sugar

2oz./50g butter
1 small egg
a few drops vanilla essence
5oz./125g self raising flour
1/2oz./15g mixed dried fruit

Grate the chocolate and chop the almonds. Cream the sugars and butter together and beat in the egg and add vanilla essence. Sift in the flour with a metal spoon and add the chocolate, almonds, and mixed fruit. Stir until all the ingredients are incorporated. Drop teaspoonfuls of mixture onto well-greased baking sheets allowing plenty of room for the biscuits to spread during cooking. Bake at 375°F/190°C/Gas Mark 5 for 10–15 minutes until golden brown.

Makes approximately 18 cookies.

GINGERSNAPS

6oz./150g self-raising flour
pinch of salt
1 tsp./5ml bicarbonate of soda
2 tsp./10ml ground ginger

4oz./100g sugar
2oz./50g lard
1½oz./40g golden syrup
1 egg

Sift flour, salt, soda and ginger together and add sugar. Melt the lard and syrup together and allow to cool slightly. Add to the dry ingredients and mix with egg to form firm dough. Divide into 24 pieces, shape into balls, and place well apart on greased baking trays. Bake at 375°F/190°C/Gas Mark 5 for about 20 minutes until a rich brown colour.

Makes 24 gingersnaps.

PEANUT COOKIES

4oz./100g demerara sugar
2oz./50g granulated sugar
3oz./75g butter
2oz./50g crunchy peanut butter
1 small egg
6oz./150g plain flour
pinch of salt

large pinch of baking powder
3oz./75g salted peanuts, chopped

Cream the demerara sugar, granulated sugar, butter and peanut butter together and beat in the egg. Sift flour, salt and baking powder together and fold into the butter mixture. Stir in the chopped peanuts. Place teaspoonfuls of mixture on ungreased baking trays, well apart to allow cookies to spread during cooking. Bake at 350°F/180°C/Gas Mark 4 for approximately 10 minutes or until the edges are light brown. Remove from trays and cool on a wire rack.

Makes approximately 36 cookies.

SCONES,
—BATTERS & PASTA—

SCONES, BATTERS & PASTA

To obtain well and evenly risen scones it is best to use plain flour with a separate raising agent. Make up a mixture using 1oz./25g cream of tartar and ½oz./15g bicarbonate of soda sifted together three times. Store in an airtight container until required. The raising power of this mixture will gradually diminish so it will be necessary to start afresh from time to time. If you're short of time you can always use self-raising flour, but the result will not be nearly as good.

1lb./400g ordinary plain
    flour
2oz./50g caster sugar
4 tsp./20ml raising agent
pinch salt
4oz./100g margarine
8fl.oz./200ml milk (use
    sour milk if available)
1 egg, beaten

Sift together the flour, sugar, raising agent and the salt; rub the margarine into the dry ingredients. Mix thoroughly to a firm dough with the milk, handling as little as possible to avoid over-kneading. Roll out using as little flour as possible to a thickness of ½ inch/12mm. Cut out circles using a plain 1½ inch/4cm cutter, taking care not to twist when doing so. Transfer the scones to an ungreased baking tray, brush tops with beaten egg. Bake at 425°F/220°C/Gas Mark 7 for 10–12 minutes. Cool on a wire rack.
Makes approximately 20 scones.

To make fruit scones add 4oz./100g sultanas to the dry ingredients and continue as above.

WHOLEMEAL SCONES

8oz./200g wholemeal flour
pinch of salt
4 tsp./20ml raising agent
2oz./50g margarine
1oz./25g lard
1oz./25g caster sugar

3–4fl.oz./75–100ml milk
    and water

Follow the method for Plain Scones.
Makes approximately 10 scones.

WHOLEMEAL CHEESE SCONES

8oz./200g wholemeal flour
pinch of salt, pepper and
    dry mustard
4 tsp./20ml raising agent

2oz./50g cheddar cheese,
    grated
3–4fl.oz./75–100ml water
1 egg, beaten

Sift all the dry ingredients together. Rub in the margarine. Stir in the cheese. Mix thoroughly to a firm dough with the water. Handle as little as possible and avoid over-kneading. Roll out and bake as for plain scones.
Makes approximately 10 scones.

RYE DROPSCONES

4oz./100g rye flour
pinch salt
2 eggs, separated
7 tbsp./140ml milk,
    approximately

Mix flour, salt and egg yolks with enough milk to make a creamy batter. Beat the egg whites stiffly and fold in. Heat and grease a griddle and make dropscones in the usual way by dropping a spoonful of the mixture onto the heated griddle and letting it sizzle and brown for 2–3 minutes on each side. Serve hot spread with butter.

Makes approximately 12 scones.

SCOTCH PANCAKES OR DROPSCONES

8oz./200g self-raising flour
pinch salt
1oz./25g caster sugar
1 egg
½ pint/250ml milk
fat for frying

Mix the dry ingredients together. Make a well in the centre and stir in the egg with enough of the milk to make batter the consistency of thick cream. Add more milk for thinner pancakes.

Drop the mixture in spoonfuls onto a hot greased griddle or heavy based frying pan. Cook for 2–3 minutes until bubbles rise to the surface of the pancakes. Turn to brown the other side and cook for a further 2–3 minutes. When cooked place on a clean tea-towel or a wire rack and cover with another clean tea-towel to retain the heat and moisture.

Serve with butter or whipped cream and jam.

Makes approximately 25 scones.

FINNISH OVEN PANCAKE

1½oz./40g butter
2oz./50g ordinary plain
    flour
pinch salt
2 eggs
½oz./15g caster sugar
8fl.oz./200ml milk

Pre-heat oven to 400°F/200°C/Gas Mark 6 and melt butter in 8 inch/20cm square baking tin. Warm the bowl and whisk while weighing out the ingredients. Sift flour and salt together. Whisk eggs and sugar until light and creamy. Add flour and milk mixing until smooth. Pour into baking tin and bake for approximately 30 minutes. Sprinkle with cinnamon and caster sugar sifted together. Cut into pieces. Serve warm with fruit preserve.

Serves 4.

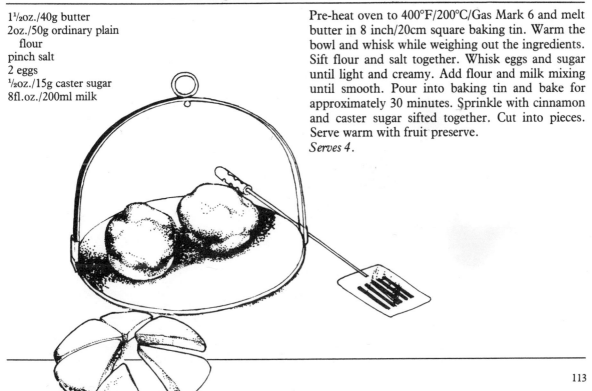

BATTERS

4oz./100g ordinary plain
   flour or wholemeal flour
pinch salt
1 egg
¼–½ pint/125ml–250ml
   milk (or milk and water)

Sift flour and salt into a bowl, make a well in the centre and drop in the egg and liquid. Beat, gradually drawing the flour into the liquid, then beat until smooth. This basic batter recipe may be varied and used as follows:

Fritters
Use ¼ pint/125ml milk to produce a batter of coating consistency. Use to coat fish, bananas, apples etc. Fry in deep fat at 190°C, until the batter is crisp and golden.

Yorkshire Pudding
Use ½ pint/250ml milk. Heat 1oz./25g dripping in a shallow ovenproof dish until very hot. Pour in the batter and bake in a hot oven, 425°F/220°C/Gas Mark 7 for approximately 30 minutes.

Baked Apple Batter
Make up batter using ½ pint/250ml milk. Heat 1oz./25g lard until smoking hot in a heatproof dish, preferably a Yorkshire Pudding tin. Peel and slice about 8oz./200g of cooking apples and place in the bottom of the dish or tin. Sprinkle 1oz./25g sultanas over the apple. Add 3oz./75g sugar to the batter and pour over the fruit. Bake as for Yorkshire Pudding. *Serves 4.*

Toad in the Hole
Use ½ pint /250ml milk and add ½ tsp./2.5ml mixed herbs, 1oz./25g chopped onion and 1tsp./5ml dried parsley to the batter. Melt 1oz./25g fat in a shallow fireproof dish and arrange 1lb./400g sausages on the bottom. Heat until the fat is smoking hot, then pour the batter over and cook as for Yorkshire Pudding. *Serves 4.*

PANCAKES

Make up batter using ½ pint/250ml milk (see page 114). Coat a thick frying pan generously with oil. Pour off the excess oil into a cup and reserve for further coatings of the pan. Add a generous table-spoon of batter to the hot pan. Tilt the pan in all directions so that the batter forms a paper thin layer. Cook for 2 minutes. Turn and cook for 1 minute on the other side.

Makes approximately 6–8 pancakes.

SMOKED HADDOCK PANCAKES

6–8 pancakes (see above)
1lb./400g smoked haddock, cooked and flaked
¼ pint/125ml double cream

salt and pepper
2oz./50g Cheddar cheese, grated
lemon wedges
1 tbsp./20ml chopped parsley

Fry the pancakes and keep warm. Mix the flaked fish with the cream and seasoning. Spread a little of the mixture on each of the pancakes. Roll up neatly and arrange in an ovenproof dish. Sprinkle over the grated cheese and brown under the hot grill. Serve sprinkled with chopped parsley and lemon wedges.
Serves 3–4.

HAM AND MUSHROOM PANCAKES

6–8 pancakes (see above)
1 onion, peeled and chopped
1oz./25g butter
4oz./100g Cheddar cheese, grated

1 tbsp./20ml chopped parsley
6oz./150g mushrooms, wiped and chopped
4oz./100g ham, chopped
salt and pepper

Fry the pancakes and keep warm. Fry the onion in a little butter. Mix half the grated cheese, with the chopped parsley, mushrooms and ham to form a paste. Season to taste. Spread a little of the mixture on each of the pancakes. Roll up neatly and arrange in an ovenproof dish. Sprinkle over the remaining cheese and bake in a hot oven 400°F/200°C/Gas Mark 6 for about 10 minutes until they are heated through and golden brown on top.
Serves 3–4.

CORNED BEEF HASH PANCAKES

6–8 pancakes (see above)
1 tbsp./20ml oil
1 onion, peeled and chopped

4 tomatoes, skinned and chopped
8oz./200g corned beef, chopped
salt and pepper

Prepare the pancakes and keep warm. Heat the oil and fry the onion until tender. Add the tomatoes and corned beef, and cook thoroughly. Spread a little of the mixture on each of the pancakes. Roll up neatly and serve.
Serves 3–4.

PRAWN AND ONION PANCAKES

6–8 pancakes (see page 115)
1 small onion, chopped
4oz./100g button mushrooms, sliced

1oz./25g butter
8oz./200g prepared prawns

Fry the pancakes and keep warm. Fry the onions and mushrooms in the butter. When tender add the prawns and fry quickly. Divide the mixture between pancakes. Roll up neatly and arrange in an ovenproof dish. Serve hot.
Serves 3–4.

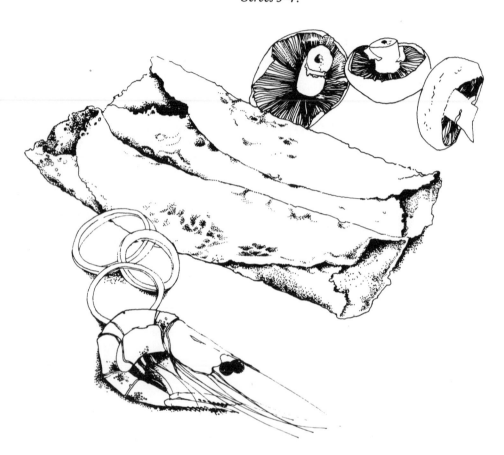

PANCAKES IN PLUM SAUCE

8 pancakes (see page 115)
2lb./800g Victoria Plums
4oz./100g caster sugar
½ pint/250ml white wine
6 tsp./30ml cornflour

Stone the plums, put into a pan with the sugar and wine, bring to the boil and simmer until fruit is tender. Drain fruit, reserving the juice, and spread over the pancakes; roll up and place in an ovenproof dish. Blend the cornflour with the reserved juice and cook until clear and thickened. Pour over the pancakes. Cover the dish with foil, bake at 400°F/200°C/Gas Mark 6 for 10 minutes.
Serves 4.

SWEET LAYERED PANCAKES

For a change make the pancakes and layer one on top of the other with one of the following fillings. Cut into wedges to serve.

1. Hot fruit pie filling.
2. Hot cooked stewed fruit drained.
3. Jam spread liberally.
4. Mashed banana and ground ginger.
5. A mixture of stewed apple and ground almonds.
Serve all with whipped cream.

CRÊPES SUZETTES

Batter
4oz./100g ordinary plain
   flour
pinch salt
1 egg
½ pint/250ml milk
1 tbsp./20ml melted butter

Sauce
2oz./50g butter
2oz./50g caster sugar
rind of 1 lemon
juice of 2 oranges
2 tbsp./40ml Cointreau
2 tbsp./40ml brandy

Mix all the batter ingredients together and beat until smooth. Leave to stand for ½ hour.

Cook the pancakes in the usual way and fold into quarters. Set aside and keep warm.

Melt the butter in the pan, add the sugar, lemon rind and orange juice; add the Cointreau, bring to the boil. Add the pancakes and simmer until heated through. Warm the brandy, pour over the pancakes, ignite and serve.
Serves 4.

TORTILLAS

Tortillas are the Mexican national pancake.

8oz./200g maize meal
8oz./200g ordinary plain
   flour

1 tsp./5ml salt
1oz./25g lard
½ pint/250ml milk and
   water

Mix the maize meal, salt and flour together, rub in the lard. Add the liquid and mix to form a dough. Leave to rest for 1 hour, covered with a damp cloth. Divide into four.

Roll each portion into a circle approximately 10 inches/25cm in diameter. Heat a large frying pan or ungreased griddle and fry the tortillas over a fairly high heat, turning them over so they are lightly browned on each side.
Makes 4.

WAFFLES

3oz./75g self-raising flour
1oz./25g cornflour
½oz./15g caster sugar
1 egg, separated

½ tsp./2.5ml vanilla
   essence
1oz./25g butter, melted
¼ pint/125ml milk

Heat and oil the waffle iron.

Sift all the dry ingredients together, add egg yolk, vanilla essence, butter and milk and mix to a smooth batter. Whisk the egg white stiffly and fold into the batter.

Spoon enough of the batter into the waffle iron to spread over the surface. Close the waffle iron and cook for 2–3 minutes until golden. Serve immediately.
Makes 6–8 waffles depending upon the size of waffle iron.

Serving suggestions:
1. Sandwich together with layers of jam, and sprinkle with icing sugar.
2. Serve with melted butter or golden syrup, or the traditional accompaniment – maple syrup.

YEAST PANCAKES

½oz./15g fresh yeast *or*
  2 tsp./10ml dried yeast
  plus ½ tsp./2.5ml caster
  sugar
½ pint/250ml milk and
  water

8oz./200g ordinary plain
  flour
½ tsp./5ml salt
½oz./15g butter
1 egg, lightly beaten

Froth the dried yeast in the warm milk and water with the sugar, *or* crumble the fresh yeast into the liquid. Sift the flour and salt together and rub in the butter. Add the yeast liquid and egg and mix until it forms a smooth batter.

Cover with a damp cloth and leave to rise in a warm place for 30 minutes. The batter should be thick and bubbly. Grease a heavy based frying pan with a little butter. Put a tablespoon of the batter into the pan and tilt around until base is almost covered. Cook over a low to medium heat until the mixture sets and the top is a mass of tiny holes and the base starts to brown. Turn over and cook until the other side browns.

Serve with butter, bacon or small sausages, or as a sweet dish with brown sugar or honey.
Makes approximately 8 pancakes.

BLINIS

These are Russian yeasted pancakes made with buckwheat flour. They are eaten with side dishes of chopped hardboiled eggs, chopped onions, chopped pickled cucumber and strips of salted herring.

¾oz./20g fresh yeast *or*
  3 tsp./15ml dried yeast
  plus 1 tsp./5ml caster
  sugar
¼ pint/125ml warm water
1oz./25g butter
¼ pint/125ml milk

1 egg, separated
8 tbsp./160ml soda water
  or fizzy mineral water
6oz./150g buckwheat flour
6oz./150g ordinary plain
  flour
1 tsp./5ml caster sugar
½ tsp./2.5ml salt
butter for frying

Dissolve the fresh yeast in the water *or* crumble the dried yeast and 1 tsp./5ml caster sugar in water and leave until frothy, about 15–20 minutes. Melt the butter in the milk, heating gently. Pour the milk and butter into the mixing bowl. Add the yeast liquid, egg yolk, soda or mineral water, sifted flour, salt and remaining sugar. Beat thoroughly until the mixture is smooth. Cover and leave for 1–1½ hours or until the batter is double in size. Whisk the egg white until stiff and fold into batter. If necessary add more water to produce a fairly thick batter of a pouring consistency.

Brush a little of the melted butter over the bottom of a heavy-based frying pan and add approximately 1 tbsp./20ml batter, depending on how thick you want the pancakes. Spread the batter thinly, using the back of the spoon, into a round of approximately 5 inches/12.5cm. Fry gently until holes appear in the surface and the base browns. Turn over and cook the other side. Wrap in a thick tea-towel to keep warm while frying remainder.

PASTA

Pasta is one of the most versatile foods; it can be made as simple or as complicated as you wish. Buy it ready made or make it yourself; serve it just with olive oil and garlic or stuff it with exotic ingredients like truffle, venison or quail.

Nowadays most commercially produced pasta is of excellent quality; in fact many Italians prefer to buy rather than make it. However, if you enjoy eating pasta the chances are that you will want to try your hand at making it sometime.

There are endless variations of the basic recipe, but this one works very well.

1lb./400g strong plain
   flour
3 eggs, beaten
1 tbsp./20ml olive oil
2 tbsp./40ml water

Sift the flour into a large bowl and make a well in the centre. Pour the liquid into the well and, using either your hands or the dough hook attachment of your mixer, gradually draw the flour into the liquid. Knead until a dough is formed; if the mixture appears to be sticky add a little more flour. Turn onto a board and knead until smooth. This will take about 2 minutes in a mixer, or 10 minutes by hand.

Cover the dough in the bowl and leave to rest for about 20 minutes. If you tried to roll at this stage, the dough would just spring back. Roll the dough out to a thickness of ⅛ inch/3mm.

Shaping of Pasta

Macaroni, spaghetti and pasta shapes like stars, shells and twists are extruded through dies commercially and are impossible to make at home unless you have a pasta extruding machine. The easiest shapes to make at home are the ribbon-like noodles which are named according to the thickness to which they are cut:

Manicotti are 3 inch/7.5cm squares.

Canelloni are 4 inch/10cm squares.

Lasagne are rectangles of any convenient size.

These should be cut from a flat sheet of dough and cooked immediately.

Tagliatelle are ½ inch/12mm ribbons.

Fettucine are ¼ inch/6mm ribbons.

Fettuce are ½–¾ inch/12–18mm ribbons.

To cut these narrow ribbon shapes, roll up a piece of flattened dough into a Swiss Roll shape. Cut slices of the correct width with a sharp knife. Unroll the ribbons and lay them flat on waxed or greaseproof paper to dry for 10–15 minutes before cooking. Any that are not required immediately should be left on the paper to dry completely. They can then be stored in paper or cardboard boxes until required. In this way pasta can be successfully stored without refrigeration: the important thing is to allow for circulation of air around it.

Any left-over pasta dough can be used to make pasta shapes. Draw the pieces together, re-roll and cut into shapes with small pastry cutters.

Filled pasta, such as ravioli should be filled, cooked and eaten without any sort of drying, which would spoil the filling.

Pasta is cooked in boiling water and it needs plenty of room in the pan. As a general rule 1lb/400g pasta requires at least 8 pints/5 litres of water plus 1 tbsp./20ml salt.

Long pasta such as spaghetti or macaroni should not be broken, but gradually lowered into the boiling water until it softens and can be coiled around the inside of the pan. All other types of pasta should be put into the boiling water at the same time, otherwise they will cook unevenly.

Commercially produced pasta takes longer to cook than the home-made kind. For cooking times follow the directions on the packet. Care must be taken not to overcook pasta. It should be what the Italians call *al dente* soft but with a bite to it, and definitely not mushy. Home-made pasta rises to the top of the pan when it is cooked; this may take anything from 2–8 minutes, so it's best to keep tasting to judge when it's ready to serve.

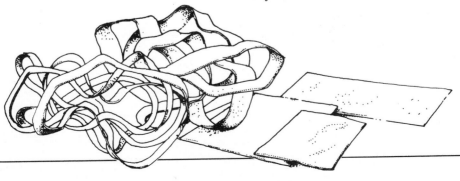

WHOLEMEAL PASTA

1lb./400g strong
  wholemeal flour
3 eggs
1½ tsp./7.5ml salt
3–6 tbsp./60–120ml water

Add the flour and salt to the liquid ingredients to form a very stiff dough. Gather the pasta together into a ball, wrap in a damp cloth or foil and allow to stand for 20 minutes. Roll out to ⅛ inch/3mm thickness. Roll up into a Swiss Roll shape and cut into ribbons about ¼ inch/6mm wide to form fettucine or other pasta shapes. Unroll and allow to dry on waxed paper. Store in a cardboard box until required.

MINESTRONE SOUP

4oz./100g pasta shapes or
  4oz./100g pasta dough
2½ pints/1.5 litres brown
  stock
2 stalks celery, washed and
  finely cut
2 large carrots, peeled and
  finely sliced
5oz./125g bacon, finely
  chopped
4oz./100g kidney beans,
  soaked overnight

basil, sage, marjoram,
  parsley, oregano to taste
1 large onion, peeled and
  thinly sliced
1 clove garlic, peeled and
  chopped
6 tomatoes, skinned and
  sliced
¼ cabbage, chopped
2 tbsp./40ml tomato purée
parmesan cheese, grated

If using home-made pasta, roll dough thinly and cut into small shapes and leave on waxed or greaseproof paper to dry. Bring the stock to the boil, add celery, carrots, cabbage, beans, herbs and bacon. Bring back to boiling point and simmer for 30 minutes. Add onion, garlic, tomato, pasta and seasoning. Simmer for 25 minutes, add tomato purée and adjust seasoning. If the soup is too thick, add more water.

Serve hot sprinkled with parmesan cheese.
Serves 6–8.

RAVIOLI NEAPOLITAN

Pasta Dough
1lb./400g plain flour made
  into pasta (see page 119)

Filling
3oz./75g cream cheese
1 egg, beaten
2 tbsp./40ml grated
  parmesan cheese
3oz./75g smoked ham,
  finely chopped

10oz./250g mozzarella
  cheese, finely chopped
parsley, chopped
salt and pepper

Sauce
2lb./1kg tomatoes, puréed
4tbsp./80ml olive oil
basil to taste
salt and pepper

To make the filling, mix the cream cheese with the beaten egg, parmesan cheese, ham, mozzarella cheese, parsley and seasoning. Divide the pasta dough into two pieces and roll out each one very thinly. Place heaped teaspoonsful of filling at 1½ inch/4cm intervals on one piece; damp the spaces between with water. Place the other piece of pasta on top and press firmly together between each bit of filling. Cut into 1½ inch/4cm squares with a pastry wheel. Cook in boiling salted water for 8–12 minutes until cooked.

Meanwhile, mix the puréed tomatoes, oil and basil together, and heat gently. Serve the ravioli in the tomato sauce with grated parmesan cheese.

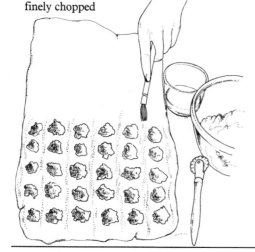

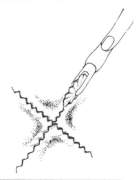

FETTUCINE WITH BACON AND ANCHOVIES

1lb./400g flour made into
fettucine (see page 119)
4oz./100g butter
2 onions, peeled and finely
chopped
2 carrots, peeled and finely
chopped
2 sticks celery, finely
chopped

4oz./100g unsmoked
streaky bacon, finely
chopped
4oz./100g lean beef,
minced
8fl.oz./200ml white wine
4 anchovy fillets, chopped
1½lb./600g tomatoes,
skinned and puréed
salt and pepper
6oz./150g parmesan cheese

Melt the butter in a pan, add the onion, carrot and
celery and cook until lightly browned. Add the bacon
and beef, and cook for a couple of minutes. Add the
wine and allow to simmer gently for 10–15 minutes to
reduce liquid, then add the anchovy fillets and
tomatoes. Mix well and continue cooking for
approximately 15 minutes.

Cook the pasta in salted, boiling water for 10–15
minutes. Drain and mix with the hot sauce. Serve hot
with parmesan cheese.
Serves 4–6.

FETTUCINE IN FRESH TOMATO SAUCE

8oz./200g wholemeal
fettucine (see page 120)

Sauce
1 large onion, peeled and
sliced
1½lb./600g tomatoes,
skinned and chopped

1 green pepper, chopped
2 cloves garlic, crushed
2oz./50g butter or olive oil
for frying
basil, rosemary
salt and pepper

Cook 8oz./200g wholemeal fettucine in a pan of
salted, briskly boiling water for 20–25 minutes until
soft.

Meanwhile heat fat and fry onion, garlic and green
pepper until tender, but do not brown. Add roughly
chopped tomatoes, seasoning, and herbs, and fry
quickly for a few moments. Drain pasta and serve hot
with the tomato sauce poured over.
Serves 4–6.

TAGLIATELLE WITH SEAFOOD SAUCE

4oz./100g tagliatelle (see
page 119)

Sauce
2oz./50g butter
1oz./25g flour
½ pint/250ml milk
1–2 tbsp./20–40ml white
wine

8oz./200g prepared seafood
(prawns, scampi,
scallops, mussels or
crab)
1oz./25g grated parmesan
cheese
salt and pepper

Cook tagliatelle in boiling, salted water for approximately 10 minutes. Meanwhile prepare a white sauce
with 1oz./25g butter and flour (see page 122), adding
the wine with the milk. Add the prepared seafood to
the sauce and heat for 5 minutes. Drain the cooked
tagliatelle and rinse in boiling water. Toss in the
remaining butter. Place in a heatproof dish, and pour
over the sauce. Serve hot sprinkled with parmesan
cheese.

Serves 2 as a main course or 4–6 as an hors d'oeuvre.

PASTA WITH PORK BALLS

1lb./400g plain flour made
into pasta shapes (see
page 119)
1lb./400g pork, minced
2 eggs, beaten
8 tbsp./160ml parmesan
cheese, grated

6 tbsp./120ml thick cream
1–2 tbsp./20–40ml
chopped parsley
5oz./125g butter
nutmeg, grated
salt and pepper

Mix the minced pork with the parmesan cheese and the eggs to form a paste. Roll into about 16 small meatballs.

Melt 2oz./50g butter in a pan, add salt and pepper and the parsley and fry meatballs until golden. Meanwhile, cook the pasta; drain, season with nutmeg and black pepper and keep warm. Melt the remaining butter and mix with the cream; add to the pasta together with the juices from the frying pan, toss together and serve with meatballs, and parmesan cheese.

Serves 4.

LASAGNE VERDI

Pasta
8oz./200g strong plain
flour
1 large egg, beaten
1½oz./40g spinach, puréed
1 tsp./5ml salt

Filling
1oz./25g butter
6oz./150g bacon chopped
2 onions, peeled and finely
chopped
1 clove garlic, peeled and
chopped
2 carrots, peeled and finely
chopped

2 celery sticks, finely
chopped
1lb./400g lean minced beef
8oz./200g chicken livers,
chopped
1 pint/500ml stock
½ pint/250ml white wine
6 tsp./30ml concentrated
tomato purée
seasoning

White Sauce
2oz./50g margarine
2oz./50g flour
1 pint/500ml milk
seasoning
parmesan cheese

Prepare the pasta by mixing all the ingredients together to form a soft dough, adding extra liquid if necessary. Roll out very thinly and cut into suitable sized pieces to fit your dish.

Cook the pasta immediately (*don't* allow it to dry out) in boiling salted water for about 5–10 minutes.

For the filling, brown the bacon in butter, then add onion, garlic, carrot and celery. Add the beef and chicken livers and cook until brown. Add stock, wine, seasonings and tomato purée. Cover and simmer for 30–40 minutes. Remove lid and if necessary reduce the liquid by fast boiling to form a thickened sauce.

Make up the white sauce by melting the margarine in a pan and stirring in the flour off the heat to form a roux. Keeping the pan off the heat, beat in the milk bit by bit. Return to heat and cook, stirring all the time, until the sauce thickens. Season to taste.

Fill a greased ovenproof dish with layers of lasagne, meat and white sauce, finishing with a layer of white sauce.

Sprinkle with parmesan cheese. Bake at 400°F/200°C/Gas Mark 6 for 20–30 minutes or until the top is crisp and bubbly.

Serves 4–6.

CANNELLONI

8oz./200g cannelloni (see page 119)

Filling
1oz./25g butter
1 onion, peeled and finely chopped
1 carrot, peeled and chopped
1 stick of celery, chopped
1lb./400g lean raw beef
3oz./75g pork sausage meat
3fl.oz./75ml white wine
½ pint/250ml meat stock
1 tbsp./20ml tomato purée

3oz./75g breadcrumbs
2oz./50g grated parmesan cheese
2 eggs, beaten
salt and pepper
grated nutmeg (optional)
1 tbsp./20ml oil

Sauce
1oz./25g margarine
1oz./25g flour
1 pint/500ml milk
1oz./25g parmesan cheese, grated
salt and pepper

Place the cannelloni on a tea-towel and allow to dry at room temperature for 3–4 hours but do not turn.

For the filling melt the butter and brown the onion, carrot and celery; add the beef, leaving it in one piece, and sausage meat. Cook gently for 10 minutes, add the wine, stock and tomato purée. Put into a greased casserole dish and cook in the oven at 325–350°F/170–180°C/Gas Mark 3–4 for approximately 2 hours until the meat is tender. Remove from the oven and allow to cool.

Drain off and reserve the liquid from the meat and vegetables. Mince the meat and vegetables and add the liquid, together with the breadcrumbs, cheese and eggs. Season to taste.

Put the cannelloni squares into boiling salted water to which 1 tbsp./20ml oil has been added. Bring back to the boil and cook for 5 minutes. Remove the cannelloni squares one by one, drain and allow to cool slightly. Place the squares on a flat surface and put some of the filling down the centre of each. Roll up and put into a well-buttered ovenproof dish with the folded edge underneath.

Make up the white sauce (see page 122). Pour over the cannelloni, sprinkle with a little more parmesan cheese and cook at 400°F/200°C/Gas Mark 6 for 15–20 minutes.
Serves 4–6.

TAGLIATELLE IN EGGS AND BACON

1lb./400g wholemeal flour made into tagliatelle (see page 119)
1 tbsp./20ml oil
6 slices streaky bacon
2 eggs, beaten

4oz./100g parmesan cheese, grated *or* hard cheese, grated
2 tbsp. chives, chopped
1 tbsp./20ml cream (optional)
black pepper

Cook pasta in rapidly boiling, salted water, to which 1 tbsp./20ml oil has been added, for 10–15 minutes. Chop the bacon and cook in saucepan until fat is melted and beginning to crisp. Add tagliatelle and mix with bacon over a very low heat. Add beaten eggs, cheese, chives, cream and black pepper. Mix well so all pasta is coated with egg and cheese. Serve immediately with more grated cheese.
Serves 4.

MANICOTTI

1lb./400g plain flour made into manicotti (see page 119)

8oz./200g ricotta cheese
2 eggs, lightly beaten
4oz./100g ham, minced
4oz./100g parmesan cheese, grated
2 tbsp./40ml mixed herbs
2 tbsp./40ml chopped chives
salt and black pepper

tomato sauce (see page 120)

Roll out the pasta dough thinly and cut into 3 inch/7.5cm squares. Allow to dry on a tea-towel for 3–4 hours. Do not turn. Cook the manicotti in salted boiling water, to which 1 tbsp./20ml oil has been added, for approximately five minutes or until soft and *al dente*. Drain manicotti and place on tea-towel. Prepare filling by combining the ricotta cheese, eggs, ham, parmesan, parsley and chives. Mix well and season to taste. Place manicotti squares on flat surface and put some of the filling down the centre. Roll up and put in a greased ovenproof dish with the folded edge underneath. Prepare tomato sauce and pour over manicotti and cook at 400°F/200°C/Gas Mark 6 for 15–20 minutes.
Serves 4–6.

FETTUCINE WITH CHICKEN LIVERS

1lb./400g plain flour, made into fettucine (see page 119)
4oz./100g butter
1 medium onion, chopped
½lb./200g mushrooms, sliced

1oz./25g flour
salt and black pepper
1lb./400g chicken livers
4fl.oz./100ml white wine
2fl.oz./50ml water

Heat the butter in a large frying pan until just melted, add the onion and mushrooms and fry until the onion is transparent. Stir in the 1oz./25g flour and season with salt and pepper. Chop the chicken livers in half and roll in flour and add to the onion and mushrooms. Cook until the livers are golden brown. Stir in the wine and water. Cook over a low heat for a further 5–10 minutes until the chicken livers are cooked. Adjust the seasoning. Meanwhile cook the fettucine in salted boiling water for approximately 10 minutes. Drain and serve the chicken livers over the fettucine. *Serves 4.*

SPAGHETTI BOLOGNESE

1lb./400g spaghetti

Sauce
3 tbsp./60ml oil
1 medium-sized onion, chopped
1 stick celery, chopped
1 carrot, diced
1 clove garlic, crushed
2oz./50g mushrooms, chopped
1lb./400g minced beef
1 tbsp./20ml flour
¼ pint/125ml red wine
1 bay leaf
1 (8oz./200g) can tomatoes, drained and chopped
2 tbsp./40ml tomato purée
½ tsp./2.5ml dried marjoram
½ tsp./2.5ml dried basil
½ tsp./2.5ml sugar

Heat oil in a large frying pan. Fry onion, celery, carrot, garlic and mushrooms until onion is transparent. Add mince and cook until all the meat is browned. Spoon off any excess fat and stir in flour. Add wine and bay leaf and bring sauce to simmering point. Add tomatoes, tomato purée, herbs and sugar and season to taste. Continue simmering, stirring occasionally, for 30 minutes. Remove bay leaf before serving.

While the sauce is simmering, cook the spaghetti. Drain and place on a warm serving dish. Tip the bolognese sauce over the pasta. Serve with grated parmesan cheese.
Serves 4–5.

SPAGHETTI WITH GARLIC SAUCE

1lb./400g spaghetti

Sauce
2oz./50g margarine
4 tbsp./80ml oil
4 cloves garlic, peeled and crushed
2 tbsp./40ml chopped parsley

1 tsp./5ml dried basil
1 tsp./5ml dried oregano
salt and black pepper
parmesan cheese

Cook spaghetti in salted boiling water for 10–15 minutes.

Meanwhile, melt the margarine in a heavy-based saucepan, add the oil and heat. Add garlic and fry until lightly browned. Stir in herbs and seasoning and remove from heat. Drain spaghetti and add to garlic sauce. Mix well and heat through. Serve with grated parmesan cheese.
Serves 4.

INDEX

Suppliers of wheat and flour

Most of the grains and flours used in these recipes may be obtained from large supermarkets and health food shops.

The companies listed below will be able to supply, and answer queries on, the more unusual grains and flours.

Allison Ltd,
Queen's Mills,
Aire Street,
Castleford,
Yorkshire
Castleford 556277

Ceres Grain Shop,
269 Portobello Road,
London W11
01-299 5571

Cranks Whole Grain Shop,
37 Marshall Street,
London W1
01-439 1809

Harmony Foods,
1 Earl Cottages,
London SE1
01-237 8396

W Jordan and Son Ltd,
Holme Mills,
Biggleswade,
Bedfordshire
Biggleswade 312001

Prewett's Mill,
Worthing Road,
Horsham,
Sussex
Horsham 3208